LOSING *Her* FINDING *Us*

*A Mother's Fight, A Daughter's Journey,
and the Road to Recovery*

Janelle Martin

Published by hope*books
2217 Matthews Township Pkwy
Suite D302
Matthews, NC 28105
www.hopebooks.com

hope*books is a division of hope*media

Printed in the United States of America

First paperback edition.

Paperback ISBN: 979-8-89185-307-2
Hardcover ISBN: 979-8-89185-231-0
Ebook ISBN: 979-8-89185-232-7
Library of Congress Number: 2025937897

ADVANCE PRAISE FOR
LOSING HER, FINDING US

"I am so honored to get a chance to endorse Janelle's book, *Losing Her, Finding Us: A Mother's Fight, A Daughter's Journey and the Road to Recovery*. Having spent 49 years working in the recovery field, I don't remember reading a more powerful presentation of the coordinated walk of a family to substance use disorder recovery. In addition, this book displays the Alternative Peer Group Program (APG) approach to recovery in all its power. Any member of this present Western world culture who gets the opportunity to read this book is truly blessed, as we are all, one way or another, suffering from this disease and could use the answers the APGs and this wonderful book offer."

—John Cates, MA, LCDC,
Founder of Lifeway International
Alternative Peer Group Programs

"It took incredible courage for Janelle and Regan to share their story. The mother-daughter relationship is complex on its own, but when addiction enters the picture, it adds an entirely new layer of challenge and pain. What's inspiring about their journey is that they found their way through it together, and now, they're using their experience to help others. Their story is a powerful reminder that transformation is possible—and even more meaningful when it's shared."

—**Lisa Marie Shaughnessy, Author of** *Testosterone: The Next Drug Epidemic* **and Clinic Outreach Manager, Amen Clinics**

"As a parent of two sons who battled addictions, I know how it feels to be completely blindsided. *Losing Her, Finding Us* tells the story of a mother whose world came to a standstill when she received an unexpected phone message with indisputable evidence. The journey is told from both the mother's and the daughter's perspective. It will bring tears of sadness and tears of joy as you see restoration happen in organic yet intentional ways."

—**Patty L. Eaton, Mother, Parents of Addicted Loved Ones (PAL) Facilitator**

A Note to the Reader

This book contains references to addiction, trauma, abuse, and mental health struggles. Some moments may be difficult to read. Please take care of yourself as you move through these pages.

Some names have been changed or omitted to respect the privacy of those involved.

Dedication

For my daughter, Regan—
You are the bravest soul I know.
Your courage cracked open hearts, including mine.
Thank you for trusting me with your story, for surviving, and for teaching me
what true resilience looks like.
This is your story—but it's also our healing.

For my husband, Tim—

You stayed. You loved us through it all.
Our steady rock—often in the background but never forgotten.
Thank you for choosing us again and again.

For the parents who have walked this road beside me—
You held space for me when I couldn't breathe.
Your strength, your vulnerability, and your acceptance helped me survive the
unimaginable.
You are not alone, and you helped me remember that I wasn't either.

And to every parent reading this who feels afraid, broken, or hopeless—
This book is for you. You are not alone.

Table of Contents

Chapter 1
How did we get here?

BACKGROUND

It's difficult to pinpoint the exact beginning of our story. There are events that may or may not be relevant to how or why this all transpired. For now, I'll start with this. I was raised a Christian and went to church regularly most of my life. I mention this because you will see my faith throughout this story. If I lose you here, know that I really hope you will bear with me, as I do not intend to impose my beliefs on anyone else. I just simply want the fact to be known that I am a Christ-follower, and this is a significant part of my life, both before my daughter's journey with drug addiction and throughout our recovery.

We are a broken family. Regan's father and I were married for almost twelve years, and our divorce was final in 2004 when she was four years old. Her older brother, Jacob, was six. Our marriage was stable, and I thought happy until I decided at twenty-six years old that I wanted kids, and he didn't. Even though he acquiesced, our relationship, mostly his treatment of me, was never the same from the moment I became pregnant. He was repulsed by me getting "fat," and then eventually became very controlling and abusive. Regan was the main reason I made the decision to leave the marriage. Looking at her, I could not live with myself letting her grow up thinking the way her dad treated her mom was normal. I resolved that I did not want this life for her.

The divorce was a difficult and messy process involving a custody dispute. Greg even attempted to convince my parents that I was an unfit mother and asked them to testify on his behalf that our children should live with him. He must have been pretty convincing because my parents at least partially believed the things he'd told them about me until they talked to me and found out he was manipulating them. Despite many accusations and my parents' refusal to help him, he failed a drug test, and the custody matter was dropped. Our children would reside with me full-time and visit their dad every other weekend and on Thursdays during the week.

While I should have clued into what my now ex-husband was capable of, I wouldn't let myself believe it. Instead, I focused on staying in church and growing my faith, raising my kids, and finding a new direction for my life. I never envisioned becoming a single mom and felt as if I was walking through my own life with a blindfold on for the first year or two. I didn't know what was next for me, but I surrounded myself with Godly women who helped me gradually find myself again. During the years following the divorce, the kids would visit their dad regularly, as we lived about thirty minutes apart. Just as he had during our marriage, he moved several times over the next few years but remained close enough to stay involved in the kids' lives. I was lenient with visitation, and I thought we got along well. We would even occasionally eat dinner together at Pizza Shack when we would exchange the kids from one to the other.

Three years after we divorced, Regan's dad moved to Illinois for what he described as a job that "he couldn't pass up" at a small start-up company. This news shocked us all because it would mean leaving his children. Regan and her brother were confused and devastated. I was angry. We had no other family in Texas, and he was my only source of support for raising our children. He told the kids first and then had a short conversation with me. I made him promise he would not abandon our kids as he had his first son, who was being raised in Kentucky by his mother and stepdad, without contact from his dad. Even though he promised me he would remain as active as he could in their lives, I could not wrap my head around him leaving his children and moving out of state. A pattern of behavior was noted, but I didn't yet know what the repercussions would be for my kids. I consoled them the best I could, but struggled to answer them when they asked me why he was moving so far away. All I could say was, "He must think this is the right thing to do." I had no answers.

To facilitate visits from their dad and to help make them less costly for him, I invited him to stay at my home with the kids on the weekends he would come to Texas. I packed up and went to a friend's for the weekend so they would have time together, just the three of them. This happened several times, and I was happy he was holding up his end of our bargain by visiting regularly. But within a few months, I met someone, and that changed everything. Tim and I started dating early in 2008, and as we grew more serious, he was the first and only man I ever introduced to my children. Complicating things, he wasn't comfortable with my ex-husband staying in my house, and I had to respect that I probably wouldn't be okay with that either if the situation were reversed. I let my ex-husband know that he would have to find other accommodations during his visits.

Later that spring, I introduced the two men when my ex-husband came to pick up the kids for a visit. Both were cordial, but at that moment, I felt the earth shift a little. My intuition was telling me something was off, but I could not put my finger on what it was, as the meeting had actually gone pretty well. Tim thought so, too, when we talked about it later. "I'm just being paranoid," I rationalized.

Tim and I got married later that year on a beach in Hawaii with the kids as our attendants. Regan was eight, and her brother was ten. Being a step-parent is not an easy job, and we won't even try to tell you we got it all right. However, Tim always wanted the best for my kids and was a constant in our home and in our lives. He never tried to take the place of their dad and, at times, stayed at arm's length to ensure this. From my perspective, Tim was imperative to Regan's childhood since her dad had moved away. He was very involved in her activities, coaching her softball teams and cheering her on in volleyball, often being the only dad attending games and tournaments. He was there for her, and I absolutely appreciated that. While he had an easier relationship with Regan, as she was younger when he came into the picture, his relationship with my son was always very strained and tension-filled.

We noticed pretty soon after Tim moved in with us that my son was not warming up to him as his sister had. He was polite and well-behaved, but pointedly distant and preferred to talk to me about anything he needed, at times ignoring Tim to converse with me only. I found this behavior odd and disappointing, but I also knew that he was going through a big change with having a new man in his life. I wanted to give him time to adjust. I truly thought he would come around, but he never really did. We had moments of peaceful connection, but the wall would always go right back up again. The tension was constant, and I could feel it in my bones when my son and my husband were in the same room together. I felt compelled to be on alert, as if something bad was going to happen, and kept myself in the middle of them just in case. My role became keeping the peace at all costs to protect them both from doing anything to create more friction with the other.

Over time, I began to realize my kids' dad was involved in creating tension and discord in our home. I didn't know what was happening exactly, but every time they came home from a visit to Illinois, my son was angry and struggled to reintegrate into our family life. He would cry a lot and avoid us by not talking and not coming out of his room except to eat or go to school. The phone calls with his dad became constant—up to twelve calls every day. He would be on the phone with his dad constantly when he was at home, which further isolated him from us. Regan seemed to be her normal self, and she also expressed confusion and concern for her brother's behavior, but their relationship was always very close. They were two peas in a pod and adored each other. I consoled myself with this fact and loved watching them act goofy together. It was in those moments that I saw my son's real personality emerge—Regan could always bring him out of his shell when they were together.

Things progressed, and we lived in a tension-filled home as if it were normal after a while. I'm certain we were all well aware of it, but felt powerless to do anything about it and afraid to do or say anything to make it worse than it was. As the kids grew older, I started to notice they would say things their dad had presumably told them about me that weren't true. He was uninvolved in parenting decisions and would tell them he was "sorry they had to deal with me" when they would convey being in trouble or having consequences. Later, through a secret phone he provided to my son, I would find messages that broke my heart. They used this phone to talk about me, call me names, and plot out the steps my son should take to live with his dad in Illinois. My intuition from years before had been confirmed in the worst possible way.

Within weeks of finding this secret phone, three weeks before my son's fifteenth birthday, I was served with papers from my ex-husband. He was suing me for custody of the kids, and to add insult to injury, he made it an emergency, alleging that the kids were being mistreated.

The process of going through a custody battle with a fifteen-year-old and a thirteen-year-old was brutal. Regan knew immediately that this entire thing was all about her brother, and she was collateral damage. On her thirteenth birthday, she met with a court-appointed attorney (amicus) after school—someone assigned to represent both her and her brother—to answer questions and share how everything had affected her. And it affected her greatly. One of my most vivid memories during that time was her returning from a visit with her dad and her brother, where they'd spent the night in a hotel. She was treated as if she weren't part of their club, as an afterthought. She came home, sat on her bed, and cried, asking me, "Why does Dad love Jacob more than me?" Seeing her understand what was really going on tore me up inside. I fought back tears of my own, honestly not knowing how to answer her. I tried to reassure her that her dad loved her. But did he? I wasn't even sure at that point.

The custody suit dragged on for a few agonizing months, but ultimately, the amicus decided in my favor. He was able to decipher what was going on by the severely conflicted emotions my son exhibited, my daughter's brokenness, and my ex-husband's manipulation. He called it "parental alienation" and wished Tim and me an ominous "good luck" in his letter to me detailing his opinion submitted to the court. As relieved as I was that it was over and the kids would remain with me in Texas, my joy was short-lived. For a little while, things improved—I think we all felt a sense of relief, even my son. But before long, the tension and heaviness crept back in.

Ultimately, Regan was blamed for refusing to go along with her dad and brother's plans, branded a traitor in her own family. The shift was sudden and cruel—one moment, she and Jacob were inseparable, and the next, he had turned on her completely. Their once-close bond deteriorated into something unrecognizable, laced with resentment, anger, and, at times, outright cruelty. She had always looked up to him and always wanted his approval, but now, he treated her like an enemy.

The day after Jacob's high school graduation, he left for Illinois, and within a few months, he cut off all contact with me. There was no conversation, no closure—just silence where my son used to be. Throughout all of these years, my ex-husband's relentless efforts to undermine me left me in a constant state of tension. I was always bracing for the next attack. His words and actions chipped away at me, leaving me feeling helpless and constantly under fire. And yet, I refused to let his bitterness consume me. I focused on my kids and reminded myself daily that the way I lived my life would speak louder than any defense I could offer.

The house we live in was purchased for the kids and me in 2004, and it is the home Tim and I live in to this day. We live in a suburb northwest of Houston, Texas, called Magnolia. Magnolia, the town, is small, but the area it spans covers several miles and is separated into "Old" and "New" Magnolia, with each possessing one of the two high schools and a population of about 138,000 people. Our subdivision is located in "Old Magnolia." Both kids went to their respective local public schools and participated in activities of their choice. We live in a quiet, gated community in a modest home with a wraparound porch (and a porch swing) that sits on a one-acre corner lot, and we survive on a modest income—neither rich nor poor. We vacationed often, sometimes together as a family, and other times, Tim and I would vacation while the kids were visiting their dad. Both kids got their licenses at sixteen and hand-me-down cars to drive. We are decidedly, blandly, middle-class. Comfortable, but not too comfortable. Both Tim and I are college-educated. I chose to work minimally outside the home while my kids were growing up, prioritizing being present for them. When Jacob reached his junior year of high school, I took a job with more hours, but it was still flexible enough to ensure I could support their activities and never miss important moments. I was always a mom first.

I'm an avid scrapbooker and have documented my life and my kids' lives from pre-birth through today in over forty-one scrapbooks. For me, it's evidence of how deeply invested I am in my family. Reliving the good moments through pictures and memories has been therapeutic and brings me so much joy.

In our home, we made it a rule that each child choose a sport or activity to participate in—not to raise professional athletes, but to give them something meaningful to work toward. We believed it would help them build skills, develop character, and stay focused, leaving less time for risky behaviors. Volleyball became a big part of all of our lives once Regan was around age twelve, and Tim and I loved watching her play. She surprised us with her athletic ability, and we supported her in every way we could—traveling to tournaments in places like Dallas and Denver, where she made close friends with her teammates. Volleyball became a reprieve for both of us, offering something fun and positive to focus on that was all about Regan. Her dad, however, never saw her play any sport at any age.

Similarly, we prioritized family dinners, eating together as often as possible, even during the busy teen years. Bedrooms were meant for sleeping, so TVs weren't allowed, and cell phones were introduced early so the kids could communicate with their dad. However, smartphones didn't come into the picture until Regan was in junior high when she received her first hand-me-down iPhone in eighth grade. At the time, I fully trusted her to use it responsibly—a decision that, in hindsight, might not have been my wisest. Back then, concerns like drugs or other risky behaviors weren't even on my radar.

Looking back, these routines and rules were my way of trying to create a stable, loving environment for my children—a foundation they could rely on no matter what challenges came our way. Volleyball, family dinners, and even the small decisions, like keeping TVs out of bedrooms, were all pieces of a bigger picture: my commitment to giving them a safe and supportive home. I wanted them to know they were loved and cared for, even when life wasn't perfect. But despite my best intentions, no rule or tradition could prevent the fractures that began to form in our family. Regan's volleyball games brought us moments of joy, but they couldn't shield her from the emotional toll of the division she felt. The same was true for Jacob—while I tried to instill a sense of security and connection, he was being pulled further away by forces outside my control.

In hindsight, I realize that even with the best parenting, there are no guarantees. Life is messy, relationships are complex, and sometimes, the things we think will hold us together aren't enough to keep us from breaking apart. As much as I tried to hold my family close, I was beginning to see the cracks I couldn't repair on my own.

REGAN'S BACKGROUND—HER PERSPECTIVE

Regan's perspective is an essential part of this book. As parents, we often long to understand what's going on in our child's mind during these struggles. To capture her experiences as accurately as possible, I conducted a series of recorded, interview-style conversations with her. These were transcribed and adapted into the sections titled *Regan*—where you'll hear her story in her own words.

REGAN

I don't remember a time when my parents were together. From as early as I can remember, Jacob was *my person*. He was my safe place, my protector, and my best friend. We did everything together. Looking back, I can see that our relationship was probably codependent—my happiness completely depended on him being there. No matter which house we were at—Mom's or Dad's—as long as I had my brother, I felt okay. The weekly back-and-forth between their homes was just our routine. It never felt strange to me because it was all I had ever known. Jacob was the one thing that never changed.

The first crack in my relationship with my dad and brother came when I was very young—maybe four or five years old. During our weekend visits with my dad, he often spent time at the house next door, where he had become good friends with the neighbor. That neighbor had a teenage son, and I dreaded going over there. While my brother was happily distracted playing video games, the boy would take me into his room and sexually abuse me. I begged my brother not to leave me alone, clinging to him, but he was too excited about the games to notice or understand my fear. I never told anyone. Not my brother. Not my dad. Not my mom. I kept it locked away for years to come. What hurt the most was the overwhelming feeling that neither my dad nor my brother protected me.

Just after my seventh birthday, my dad sat my brother and me down and told us he was moving to Illinois for a new job. I don't remember feeling sad about it, but I saw the sadness in my brother's face, so I mimicked his reaction. If it was a big deal to him, then it must be a big deal to me, too. At that age, I didn't fully understand what it meant until we started having to fly on an airplane just to see him. He wasn't around as much anymore, but we would go visit him for longer stretches in the summer, at Christmas, and during spring break. It was just normal for us after a while.

A couple of months after my eighth birthday, my mom married Tim, my stepdad. The wedding was on a beach in Hawaii, but I couldn't have cared less about the ceremony—I just wanted to play in the sand and water. The wedding was really boring, but I loved Tim from the start and was happy to have him around. Some of my favorite memories are of him taking me to Chuck E. Cheese, playing games with me, and riding the little roller coaster there with me over and over again. He also coached my softball teams and provided a sense of consistency and security I didn't know I needed.

Over the next several years, my relationship with my dad started to shape how I saw myself within our family. I first noticed a shift when I was about eight years old. Gradually, there seemed to be a clear division in our family—dad's side and mom's side. By the time I was nine, I realized my dad favored my brother over me. It started with small things, like always doing what Jacob wanted to do, eating what Jacob wanted to eat, and watching the movies Jacob wanted to watch. It often felt like two against one, and I was left out a lot. One night at dinner, my dad jokingly made a comment about me gaining weight. I wanted his love and approval, so I started restricting my eating, hoping it would make me more acceptable to him.

Over time, I began to sense an unspoken, yet extreme, disappointment from both my dad and brother anytime I showed closeness to my mom and stepdad. It was like I wasn't supposed to love both sides of my family. But despite wanting to connect with my dad, I struggled to be close to him—I didn't really trust him because he wasn't around much. He was virtually absent from my day-to-day life.

For years, I wrestled with this mental tug-of-war, but when I was twelve, something happened that made everything painfully clear. During a visit to my dad's house, he had me and my brother sit down in the living room and write out reasons why we loved coming to visit him, why we wanted to live with him, and why we didn't want to live with our mom anymore. I sat there for hours, staring at a blank page, because I had nothing to write. But he wouldn't let it go.

The truth was, if I made a list comparing my parents, my mom would win. I didn't want to leave my friends. I didn't want to leave my life. I sat there, trapped, knowing I couldn't give him what he wanted. But eventually, I wrote down my honest thoughts, which favored my mom because my life and my friends were too important to me.

That same year, everything with my brother changed, too. After a trip to visit our dad for spring break, I noticed that Jacob suddenly had two cell phones. I didn't know why, but when I pointed it out, he got furious. That was the moment I became invisible to my entire family. When mom found the second phone and confiscated it, the ensuing chaos only reinforced my feelings. No one told me anything, but suddenly, everyone was fighting over Jacob and which parent was "worse". The only thing that mattered was what would happen to him. I was just... there.

The only reason I even knew what was happening was because

I went through my mom's room, found the extra phone, and read the messages inside. That's when it all hit me. The texts were filled with complaints about how much Jacob hated being at home, cruel names he called our mom—including calling her a "b****," jokes at her expense, and insults about her that made my stomach turn. Suddenly, it became painfully clear where the issues in our family stemmed from.

Not long after, my dad took my mom to court to get custody of Jacob. But it was clear—he wasn't fighting for both of us. He didn't want me. The court wouldn't split us up, so we both stayed with our mom. But the whole thing made me feel genuinely depressed. I had always suspected my dad didn't care about me or love me. Now I knew it.

After he lost the custody case, my brother's anger grew. His resentment toward my mom only intensified, and I became increasingly isolated from both Jacob and Dad. My dad seemed to give up trying to get me to choose his side, but Jacob blamed me for not going along with their plans. I was the reason he couldn't live with Dad and be happy. He was hateful. And just like that, the love, trust, and protection I had always felt from my big brother were gone.

I was thirteen years old the first time I had suicidal thoughts. I searched the house for medication to overdose on, but when I couldn't find any, I just curled up in bed and cried myself to sleep. I never told anyone how desperate or depressed I was.

The only thing that kept me going was volleyball. It was the one place where I could leave everything behind the second I stepped onto the court. I lived for that sport. It was my escape. My sanity. My life.

Chapter 2
The Start

2016

It would seem prudent to start off with when I was clued into my daughter's substance abuse. However, I feel like there are events leading up to that point that are important to the story. Not that they necessarily provide the excuse or the "why" behind it all, but maybe they provide some clues that I missed or that are relevant to how it all began.

Regan's sophomore year of high school was a tumultuous one. Her older brother, Jacob, was a senior that year and spent nine months (from the beginning of the school year to the end of it) angry at her. He punished her by shunning her, denigrating her, and glaring at her as often as he could. It was a miserable time. What did she do to deserve this treatment? Well, as a parent, I would say that *nobody* ever deserves to be treated in such an unkind way, especially someone you love.

Some situations arose early in the school year involving Regan's questionable choices and other events that seemed to happen to her despite her actions. The teen years are not for the weak; she had her share of difficulties. One such experience was when she lied about where she was staying one night, claiming to be with a friend when she was actually somewhere else entirely. The way I uncovered the truth was both accidental and mortifying after running into the friend's parent at a swim team meeting the following morning. When I saw her, my stomach instantly hurt, but I casually asked her if my daughter was still at her house. I already knew the answer by the confused look on her face. She kindly lowered her voice, telling me, "Regan didn't spend the night with us last night." She then turned to her daughter next to her and asked, "Do you know where Regan was last night?" She silently shook her head, no, and I knew my face had flushed full red with embarrassment. My mind raced with possibilities of where she might be and who she was with. *Was she okay?*

Regan answered my messages after a few minutes, knowing she was busted. She had always been terrible at lying as a child—her face would give her away instantly—so this betrayal of trust felt shocking and completely out of character for her. Tim and I went to pick her up at the address she had texted me after our meeting was over, and it was one of the hardest moments I'd experienced as her mom. Seeing where she'd spent the night was a shock, and I struggled to reconcile the image I had of her with how she ended up there. The house was rundown and in complete disarray, with junk all over the yard. The person she was with came out to see her go, but I couldn't help but wonder if there was a parent there. It didn't make sense to me, and I don't remember any of us saying much on the drive home or even after arriving home. The event spoke for itself. I was in disbelief, Tim was concerned, and Regan just went to her room.

Regan's punishment for lying was being grounded for a few

months, and we also took her phone away. We restricted social media, specifically Snapchat and Twitter, when we gave her phone back. I hoped that not having access to these apps would give her a break from the fake social media world and having to see all the friends and activities she might have been excluded from. I wanted to protect her, and I made sure we had a lot of talks about the pros and cons of social media. She survived our punishment and our lectures, but this was a pivotal moment in my understanding that something was starting to simmer under the surface.

It was difficult for her to find lasting friendships in high school, through no real fault of her own. The girls she would start to become friends with would suddenly turn on her for no apparent reason, which was not only distressing but added to her already very complicated family experiences. Each time she would find a group of friends she thought she fit in with, they would move away, or something would happen, and she would start to be left out or, worse, gossiped about in heinous ways. She didn't always tell me these things were happening to her, but I had some clues because she only talked about certain girls for a period of time before I didn't hear those names anymore. I think she tried to deal with these hurts on her own, ultimately internalizing them and trying to cope the best she could. She put on a normal, happy face at home and then went into a proverbial lion's den every day when she walked through the front doors of the high school.

Further compounding things, Regan was playing on a competitive volleyball team and had earned the libero position—a key back-row defensive role focused on serve receive and quick reflexes. Inexplicably, her coach demoted her from that position in the Nationals tournament after she had played libero all season. Her playing time was a fraction of what it had been, and the team did not do well. I know that deeply affected her, and she never understood why her coach did that to her.

A few months later, things got even worse. She quit her new indoor team mid-season after the coach pulled her aside one evening after practice. He asked her if she would be okay with giving up a significant amount of playing time so that a younger, much less skilled teammate could have more time on the court. He wanted to make it "fair" for all the girls, but at sixteen, Regan had been used to playing competitively and wasn't willing to compromise.

I panicked at the thought of volleyball not being part of her life and quickly suggested she switch to beach volleyball. She did, but it took some time for her to warm up to it, and meeting all the new girls was intimidating after all she'd been through. I didn't know if she would stick with it, but I hoped and prayed she would eventually love the sport again. She needed something that could be hers and would bring her happiness.

Her brother's treatment of her also deteriorated. Home wasn't even a respite for her. Instead of protecting her or being there for her, he treated her as if she had committed crimes for which she could not be forgiven. He glared at her and called her names every time they were in the same room. I tried talking to him, tried reasoning with him, and tried to get him to stop being so mean to her, but he refused to listen. I felt desperate and helpless to get him to see what he was doing to her, and simultaneously frantic to protect her from continuing to be beaten down. It was a very tense and sad time in our household for all of us. I know I was constantly on edge and hyper-aware of everyone's actions.

I believe it took its toll on Regan the most. She had always loved and adored her big brother, and they had been thick as thieves for their entire existence up to that point. They grew up doing everything together and loving each other like siblings should.

He protected her, and she looked up to him. Their relationship was one I was proud of. Their bedrooms were connected in much the same way as their lives were. Each had their own separate vanity leading through a pocket door to their shared tub/shower and toilet area—a Jack and Jill bath. That space, their own little wing of the house, was like a world that belonged only to them. The pocket doors weren't just a passageway; they were a private gateway that they used to plot, plan, laugh, and play for years. Those doors had always been open between them—until they weren't. His treatment of her was shocking, to say the least.

This situation came to a head in late April 2016 with a volatile fight—one witnessed by Regan's friend, who had been spending the day with her.

My husband and I were out to dinner with friends nearby when my phone rang. Seeing Regan's name on the screen, I answered as I always did when one of my kids called.

"Hello?"

She was crying. My stomach immediately clenched, and I turned to Tim, signaling that something was wrong. I stepped away from the table and asked gently, "What's wrong?"

Through choked sobs, she said something to the effect of, "Jacob hit me."

Panic set in. "What? Why?" I asked, struggling to understand her through the tears.

"He came home and started yelling at me, calling me names, and then he hit me," she managed to get out. "I don't want to be here with him, Mom. Can you and Tim please come home?"

I didn't hesitate. "We're on our way."

Tim and I left the restaurant immediately, my mind racing the entire drive. I wasn't sure what had happened, but I could hear how distressed she was. While I didn't think Jacob would seriously hurt her, I wasn't about to leave her in that situation.

We pulled into the driveway within ten minutes, barely shutting off the car before rushing inside. The sight before us stopped me cold.

Jacob was towering over Regan, inches from her face, screaming. I was so stunned that I couldn't even register what he was saying. Wide-eyed, I yelled, the only thing that came to mind.

"Stop!"

Regan was crying, yelling back at him, while her friend stood nearby, looking frightened and helpless.

Tim was right behind me. As I tried to step between them, Tim took over, turning his attention to Jacob. His voice boomed through the house. "You don't put your hands on your sister!"

Jacob snapped back at him immediately, and the argument escalated.

I tried to get between them, my hands up, begging them both, "Please, stop!"

Neither of them heard me. Their voices drowned out anything I said. I saw Tim push Jacob—once, maybe more. I had never seen Tim this angry, but he wasn't backing down. Jacob was just as defiant.

"You tried to choke me!" Jacob accused, stepping back, his eyes blazing. "I'm calling the police."

I hadn't seen Tim choke him, but I had seen them pushing each other. The whole thing felt surreal, like a scene from a movie. I turned away, needing space from the chaos. I needed air.

Regan and her friend were still in the bedroom. I went to check on them, but my heart sank when her friend quietly told me she had already called her parents to pick her up.

"I just don't feel safe around him," she admitted.

I understood. And I hated that she had been caught in the middle of this. "I'm so sorry," I told her as I awkwardly thanked her for sticking up for Regan. What was I even saying?

Before I could process any more, I heard Jacob on the phone. He had actually called the police. My body tensed, the weight of the moment pressing down on me.

He was also calling his dad, telling him what had happened between him and Tim.

Stunned, I turned to Tim. "Did he really just call the police?"

Tim nodded. "They're on their way."

I felt disoriented, my mind struggling to catch up. Flashing lights appeared through the windows, cutting through the dark. A sheriff's car pulled into the driveway, red and blue bouncing off the walls.

This isn't happening. We are not this family.

My hands shook as I pulled out my phone and called our pastor—who was also Jacob's best friend's father. I had no idea if I was even making sense, but I begged him to come help us sort this out.

"The sheriff is here," I said, my voice barely above a whisper.

"I'm on my way," he assured me.

I hung up and turned toward the door, watching helplessly as the deputy stepped out of his car.

Tim was already outside talking to him. I swallowed hard, trying to calm my racing heart.

The deputy was kind and took his time speaking with each of us separately. By the time our pastor and his wife arrived, the tension had started to ease. They each took one of us—our pastor speaking to Jacob, his wife comforting me.

Having them there grounded me in a way I desperately need-ed. I felt both gratitude and deep embarrassment.

This is what things have come to.

As I stood in my driveway, watching the flashing lights reflect off the pavement, my heart shattered.

I'm not sure how traumatic that incident was for Regan, but it was pretty traumatic for me. Jacob went home with our pastor and stayed with them for at least a week while everyone tried to decompress. He eventually apologized to his sister for the way he had treated her and then apologized to us for being disrespectful. I don't think his apology to me was very sincere, but I didn't care that much about that. My concern was that he restore, or begin to restore, his relationship with his sister, and that seemed sincere. They started to rebuild their connection, and Regan even went to his senior prom with him a couple of weeks later. They had a lot of fun, and their dynamic seemed much better.

He graduated from high school and moved to Illinois with his dad about a week later. Just like that, he was gone, and she was alone again—without her brother, just when they'd started to become close again. I remember she slept in his bed for a while after he left, as if being in his space could somehow bring him back or make the emptiness less unbearable. She missed him terribly, grieving not just the time she had lost with him but the present moment—the reality of him not being there with her now. I ached to make it easier for her—to say or do something that would take away even a fraction of her pain, but there was nothing. I thought time would help. I hoped it would anyway.

That summer, Regan threw herself into beach volleyball, spending countless hours on the sand, and we traveled nearly every weekend to tournaments in Galveston, Dallas, San Antonio, and

Houston. She even spent a week in Hermosa Beach, California, at a beach volleyball camp, an experience she genuinely seemed to enjoy. By the time September arrived, so did a milestone—her sixteenth birthday. We surprised her with a party filled with friends, laughter, a lively game of water kickball in the front yard, and plenty of pizza and cake. Things felt like they were looking up for the first time in a long time. She got her driver's license shortly after and, not long after that, started dating Trey, a boy from a neighboring town. He became her first real boyfriend, and when she wasn't playing volleyball, she was often with him.

2017

By the end of January, that relationship fell apart; simultaneously, some friendships also ended. It was a rough time for Regan, and I'm certain there are things that happened that I don't know of, but what I do know is that some girlfriends were jealous of her relationship with Trey and started a campaign against her. They told Trey behind her back that she was cheating on him and flirting with other guys at school. Believing these lies, he broke up with her. But it didn't stop there. She was not allowed to defend herself, and both her friends and Trey joined against her. I know this is probably typical teenage drama, but Regan was really devastated by it all.

She told me of one instance where the group of friends she would ride with during her child development class to a daycare where they were supposed to help out, walked with her to the school doors, and then took off running once outside, got into their car, and left her. When she told me this happened, it felt like a knife to my heart. She drove herself to the daycare that day and every day after that.

She really didn't associate too much with those girls from

school anymore. I also don't remember any new friends coming to light. It's possible she kept to herself after all that—maybe she thought it was easier to protect herself from hurt if she stayed away from people... or at least kept her distance. I wasn't fully aware of this at the time. My hope was that she would get through it and be fine. I hated high school, too—doesn't everyone?

She continued with beach volleyball, and nothing seemed really amiss that spring. She drove herself to and from her activities and her job (she was a hostess at a local Mexican restaurant) and played tournaments most weekends, determined to qualify for Nationals.

I do not know when she started experimenting with drugs. I wish I could tell you there was a moment when it was clear that she was doing something wrong. There wasn't. Even looking back, I cannot pinpoint anything that would have made me suspect drugs. It wasn't even on my radar. However, at some point here, that's what happened. My belief is that it started in May—for the first time ever, she asked if she could attend a party. It was a graduation party, and she was going with a good friend whom I had known, so I allowed her to go. She was home on time, and I was awake and heard her come in. I did not check on her or talk to her—I didn't want to be overbearing. She was growing up, and I wanted to trust her.

There was a second graduation party the next weekend that she asked to go to. Same scenario, same friend, same reaction from me. *Sure, but be home by midnight and have fun.* Drugs did not cross my mind. I think I did tell her not to drink, though—and not to ride in a vehicle with anyone who had been drinking. I would be glad to come and pick her up if she got into a situation where she needed a safe ride home. We did have that conversation, and she understood and agreed that she would do that. She came home on time again and without incident. I didn't think much of it afterward. Life went on as normal.

Summer was upon us, and we were busy with volleyball tournaments, practices, and work, and she loved to sleep in whenever she could—a normal teenager. My birthday was in mid-June, and I raised an eyebrow when she went above and beyond for my gift. She got me flowers, a very nice card, and chocolate, and said lots of really beautiful things to me. It certainly wasn't anything that made me think she was doing drugs, but I did notice that this expression was out of the ordinary, albeit very sweet. I appreciated it very much. I actually thought maybe she was making up for her brother's lack of contact with me—she always had the biggest heart.

At some point here, Regan started to mention that she wasn't enjoying volleyball practice as much. This was strange because volleyball had always been her passion—something she truly loved. She had worked hard for years, and now she was training with a private coach who specialized in developing athletes for sand volleyball. She'd always loved working with him in the past, but suddenly, things seemed different.

At first, I thought she was just being a typical teenager, complaining about early morning workouts in the middle of summer. She started making excuses—she was tired, she needed a break, she just didn't enjoy it like she used to. It was frustrating to hear because she had worked toward this for so long. I worked every day, so it was up to her to get herself to training sessions and practice. As far as I knew, she was going. Why wouldn't she? We had paid for everything, and she was still competing in tournaments nearly every weekend. It didn't make sense that she would stop training, but she kept saying she wasn't enjoying it anymore.

Looking back, I honestly don't know if she was attending her practices or not. At the time, I assumed she was. I didn't think too much of her complaints—maybe she was just burned out. Maybe she was tired of the repetition and hard work that came with serious training. But in sports, you do the drills even when you don't love them because they make you better. I suppose that's why her complaints mostly fell on deaf ears.

She finally convinced me to let her stop working with her trainer, and by the end of June, she had eliminated those sessions altogether. Volleyball practices, however, were not up for debate. She had already earned bids to compete in both the AAU and USAV Junior Nationals tournaments, and sand time was necessary if she wanted to be ready.

Tim and I made plans to spend the 4th of July weekend with some friends who had moved about an hour away. We'd been invited to drive down to their home and enjoy a relaxing time in their pool. Regan had to work and, of course, wasn't thrilled at the idea of spending an entire weekend with adults, so she declined to come with us. This was the first time we had ever made plans to leave her home alone, but she was turning seventeen soon and about to be a senior in high school, so I thought it would be okay for just one night. I did have her make arrangements to stay with a family we trusted that night, though. I didn't want her at the house alone for various reasons. She agreed to stay with her friend from volleyball that night (in a neighboring town), and I had no reason not to believe her. She was almost always very agreeable and willing to abide by my requests. I checked up on her often…. even before this weekend. She always was quick to reply to texts or phone calls—it was very rare that she didn't.

I feel compelled to mention here that she did not have a lock on her bedroom door. And I did not have a habit of knocking before coming into her room… I did this on purpose. Never once did I catch her doing anything she shouldn't have been doing, nor was I ever suspicious of anything. However, I wanted to keep the element of surprise with her… just in case. I could literally walk in on her at any time, and she was well aware of that. She never even gave me a hint that this bothered her.

Thankfully, Tim and I were with some of our closest friends that weekend. I had texted or talked to Regan that evening, trying to make sure she had gotten to her friend's house. She did finally get there, and I was pretty irritated that she'd gotten there so late—it must've been around 10 p.m. or so. I thought it was odd, but then again, she'd had the day to herself, so I didn't think too much about it. I was relieved that she was there, and then didn't think about it again.

After a quick breakfast on Sunday morning, we got up and headed outside to the pool. The guys had left the house to go flying (our friend had gotten his pilot's license), so it was just us girls left at the house. Roz, Jessica (her adult daughter), and I had a nice time chatting by the pool and soaking up the sun.

I'm not sure what time it was when I got the message through Facebook Messenger. When I opened it, I thought I might die. I could not speak. I could only stare and feel like I was being buried alive under a mountain of rocks. We live in a fairly small town, which basically means that we know lots of people. Some better than others, of course, but my circle is wider than it might appear. The message was from a classmate of Regan's. She had gone to school with Regan her whole life, but they had never really been friends. This girl's mother used to work for me when our girls were toddlers, and ironically, I had seen them both at the Dollar Store within months of that day, and we had had a conversation about lots of things. Carly was into pageants, and she'd had a boyfriend that she'd broken up with recently, because he was a drug user. She was pursuing modeling and competing in pageants, and her mom was her biggest support and cheerleader. It was nice to see them and nice to catch up a bit.

This message from Carly was quite a surprise. She'd sent a photo captured from a Snapchat story or post of Regan with some sort of thing on her tongue... was it a pill? A paper? I wasn't sure, but I knew it wasn't good. In the photo, she was riding in a vehicle, and the driver was Carly's ex-boyfriend. Red flag. Carly's message was one of concern for Regan:

```
hey so i know this isn't really my
business and i don't wanna start
any trouble.. but i've noticed Re-
gan is starting to hang out with
the wrong crowd and posted this
picture on snapchat of her do-
ing LSD..i know this boy person-
ally because he's my ex boyfriend
and he's nothing but trouble he's
hot wired cars, stole hundreds of
dollars and sells lots of differ-
ent drugs and i don't really want
Regan knowing it's me telling you
this just because i've known her
all my life but i don't wanna
see her get into trouble that she
can't get out of
```

She next sent me this when I didn't answer:

```
I'm sorry if I caused offense or
trouble, but I just don't want
anything bad to happen or her to
```

get hurt

I truly appreciated that and told her I would not tell Regan who told me, and that she could reach out to me anytime about anything, and I would protect her. Then she told me more:

> Thank you, this has been going on for quite a while actually…she's posted videos of both of them smoking weed at his house before, but once I saw the picture of her doing LSD, I felt like I had to say something just because of how dangerous it is

Wow. I was stunned. I could not breathe for a bit. Most of these words did not resonate with me; they seemed to bounce off me. I thought I might crumple into a heap. As I politely typed out a thank-you to Carly for the information and for caring about my daughter enough to tell me, I tried to stop my hands from shaking. I'm sure the look on my face was pure panic as my friend asked me what was wrong. I could not say the words out loud to her, so I said I needed to make a phone call and proceeded into the house and out the front door for some privacy. Still in disbelief at the photo on my phone, I wanted to get rid of it. I wanted not to have seen it. I wanted this to be a joke or at least a huge mistake. Surely, this wasn't really happening. She knows better! How in the world? At some point, our husbands had returned from their flight, all happy and ready for some pool time. I pretended to be happy to see them and interested in their experience, but I was in a daze. I needed to call my daughter. NOW.

As the call was going through, I became angry. What was she thinking? DRUGS? REALLY? I was determined to scare some sense into her. She answered, and I immediately said, "What in the world are you doing?" as if she knew that I knew. She didn't. She mumbled something, and I barely let her finish. I am sure I said something to the effect of, "Who were you with yesterday and what were you doing?" I think she knew she'd been caught, but she did not know to what extent. I told her someone had sent me a photo of her, so she'd better not try to lie about it. She started to cry and got very quiet. She didn't have much to say for herself, and I was livid at that point. However, instead of hashing it out over the phone in my friend's front yard, I told her we'd be home in a few hours, and we would be discussing this in detail then. She was instructed to remain at home and to be ready to talk. Oh, how I dreaded going home that day. And I dreaded going back to the backyard and pretending everything was okay as we finished our pool time with our friends. I felt sick to my stomach.

I did go back to the pool, forcing a smile as I rejoined our friends, but the cool water did nothing to settle the heat rising in my chest. Laughter echoed around me, splashes of carefree joy filling the air, but I felt miles away. My body was there, but my mind was elsewhere—trapped in a loop of worst-case scenarios, fear pressing against my ribs like a vice.

I tried to engage, to push the thoughts away, but they kept clawing their way back. *What am I going to say to Tim?* The very thought made my stomach twist. He was going to be mad. My hands curled into fists beneath the water. I hated it when he got like that, when his voice hardened and frustration lined his face. But I needed his help. I didn't want to do this alone. *I couldn't do this alone.*

The fun around me became nothing more than background noise. My limbs felt heavy, my breathing shallow. The weight of what I had to face gripped me from head to toe, cold and unrelenting. I had to go.

Water dripped from my skin as I pulled myself out of the pool, my towel wrapped around my shoulders like a shield. I didn't offer an explanation, just a quick, distracted goodbye. My only thought was getting home—*getting to her*. The fear was suffocating now, wrapping itself around my chest, stealing my breath.

My mind continued to race. I've never even tried drugs... never even tried cigarettes... never was even tempted to do any of that. We had watched season after season of *Intervention* on TV to show the kids what drugs will do to a person—they never glamorized it. It was always a train wreck. Did she not remember that? Did she not pay attention? This really could not be happening. We had about an hour drive home from our friends' house. It was excruciating. I spilled the beans to Tim pretty quickly after getting in the car and showed him the photo.

He wasn't mad. I had expected him to react emotionally, just as I had, but instead, he stayed calm, taking in everything I was saying. Looking back, I think he did it for my benefit—knowing I was breaking apart inside and wanting to hold me together. He was disappointed in her, but also didn't want to jump to conclusions without more information. We talked through scenarios of what we thought might be going on with her. He'd tried pot and other drugs when he was a teenager, so he suggested that she was likely just experimenting and it would pass... like a phase. However, he was firm with me that we would not allow drug use in or near our home. We also wanted to be clear that we did not condone drug use at all, under any circumstances, and that she was to stop. He was less concerned than I was, and that made me feel better. I hoped he was right. She was just being a normal teenager. This wasn't as serious as I was making it out to be. Please, God, let this not be the worst thing in the world

REGAN

I don't remember a whole lot from this time, but I do remember the first time I tried marijuana. It was shortly after my breakup with my boyfriend, early in the second semester of my junior year. A friend introduced me to it, and at that point, everything had accumulated—my friendships had fallen apart, school was miserable, my relationship ended, and my brother was gone. I had no sense of security anywhere. I couldn't turn to my parents because of all the family s***. I couldn't turn to my brother because he wasn't there. I had zero friends to rely on. So I thought, *What do I have to lose?* At that point, why not?

Almost immediately, all the pain I had been carrying—the heartbreak, the loneliness, the depression—it all lifted off me, almost like it floated into the air and just disappeared. The weight that had been suffocating me was gone. For the first time in what felt like forever, I could breathe. And in that moment, I realized: *I don't have to live with this pain. I can use drugs, and it's just gone.* I didn't hate myself. I didn't hate my life. I didn't want to die. It was like flipping a switch—one minute, I was drowning in everything, and the next, I felt happy. I felt like I didn't have to fake it anymore.

A week later, I tried LSD for the first time. I was still smoking every day, but that night, I did Xanax too—just to sleep, because acid keeps you awake. It probably wasn't normal to escalate that quickly, but when it was offered to me, I didn't hesitate. The first time had been so good, I thought, *f*** it.* I didn't see any downside. When the high wore off after that first week, reality came crashing back, and I realized how miserable I actually was. So, when more drugs were offered to me, I was excited. I didn't care what it was—I just wanted the pain to turn off again.

After that, smoking became an everyday thing. Marijuana, sometimes Xanax, sometimes acid. I was still functional, still careful—never before practice, never before something important—but I was high all the time. And the thing about weed is, when you use it as often as I did, you build a tolerance. I could smoke, get high, and an hour later, it would wear off. So I wasn't walking around completely out of it—I was just doing enough to take the edge off, to give me that glimpse of happiness that made life feel bearable.

Volleyball had been the one place where I could escape everything, but even that started slipping away. My tolerance for drugs had grown, and getting high didn't last as long anymore, which only made me want to use more. At first, volleyball was my safe place—the one thing that could quiet my mind. But then, I'd be at practice and couldn't get out of my head. Instead of being an escape, it became another source of stress. I felt like I couldn't focus, like I was screwing up constantly, and my coach was always on my ass. I started dreading it.

I think losing Jacob hurt me more than anything else. Not just when he treated me horribly, but when he left. When he was here, even if he was awful to me, he was still *here*. But when he was gone, I felt like he took a part of me with him. I don't know why I loved him so much, but I did. He could've stabbed me and put me in the hospital, and I don't think I would've held it against him. I don't remember much from that time—not even because I was high, just because I think my brain blocked it out for me.

Chapter 3
Use Continues...

As I pulled into the driveway, a wave of anger rolled through me, tightening my chest. The thought actually crossed my mind—pack her bags, throw them on the porch, and make her leave. *I'm not okay with drugs. She HAS to know that.* The betrayal stung, but underneath the anger was something much heavier. Fear.

I don't remember if I took my suitcase inside first or went straight to find her. But somehow, we ended up outside, sitting on the wooden bench on the front porch. The air was thick with humidity, the kind of suffocating heat that comes with July in South Texas. It didn't make sense to be out there, but maybe we just didn't waste time getting the conversation started.

I turned to her, my voice sharper than I intended. "What in the world are you doing?"

She mumbled something I couldn't make out, and then, just like that, the tears came. Silent at first, then in shaky sobs. I knew she hated anyone being upset with her—especially me. But this wasn't just about disappointing us. This was something deeper.

Through her tears, she admitted it—marijuana and ecstasy. "Nothing else, Mom." Her voice wavered. She looked away. Could I believe that?

"I'm just… I'm sad," she finally confessed. "There's no way I'm going back to school at Magnolia West. I hate that place."

My mind reeled. *This is about school? Or is it about something else?* The pieces weren't fitting together, but before I could press further, Tim stepped in.

"Whatever you want, we'll figure it out," he said firmly. "But you have to quit using drugs, Regan. No more."

She nodded, but it wasn't exactly reassuring.

"We'll find you a different school," I added, my voice softer now, trying to catch up with what was happening. "And I know a counselor you can talk to. I'll call her after the holiday."

She nodded again, wiping her face with the back of her hand. Then, almost hesitantly, she said, "I really want a dog."

I exhaled. *A dog?* She had always wanted one, but with sports and travel, we had never been able to make it work. But now… now it felt like a lifeline. Something to ground her.

"Okay," I said. "We'll get you a dog."

"We'll do all of this," Tim added, "but there will be NO drugs, Regan. If you keep using, you can't live here."

"Okay," she whispered.

I searched her face, hoping for some sign of conviction, some promise that she would stop. But she didn't say the words. She didn't *promise* anything. Still, it seemed that agreeing to these things made her feel better. It made us feel better, too. After all, we were doing something about this. We ended the conversation by hugging her, assuring her that we loved her and only wanted the best for her.

She was supposed to play at the USAV National Beach Volleyball tournament in Siesta Key in just a couple of weeks. We debated on not letting her go... after all, there should be punishment for using drugs! However, in beach volleyball, you play with only one partner, so if we didn't go, then it would also have penalized her partner. We didn't want to do that. And I really didn't want to have to tell anyone what was going on. If we canceled, they would be owed a plausible explanation. What kind of parent would I look like if I told them Regan couldn't go to Florida to play at Nationals because she was using drugs? There was no way I was going to tell anyone that! We'd go and hope she had learned her lesson by getting caught. We were already doing what we thought would rectify the situation anyway. Nationals is a big deal... she'd earned that opportunity, and maybe it was just what she needed to pull her out of her sadness.

I feel compelled to note here that I did not call Regan's dad to tell him what was going on. It crossed my mind, but I dismissed it. After a failed attempt at gaining custody of our kids in 2013, he'd pretty much refused any contact or communication with me unless it had to do with the kids visiting him... and even then, it was minimal, or he'd try just going through the kids and avoiding me altogether. My son had followed his lead and hadn't spoken to me in a year as well (he was eighteen at this time). Given the situation, I debated whether to tell him and decided against it because he lived out of state, and what was he really going to do? Ground her? Tell her something we hadn't? It's pretty hard to do real parenting over the phone. Plus, telling him seemed like I'd be handing him a golden opportunity to make this my fault, like he had done multiple times (with much less serious situations) in the past. I didn't tell him because he wasn't here and couldn't really help, but mostly, I didn't tell him because surely it would have given him ammunition to use against me to feed into his "good cop, bad cop" routine. Nope. I would handle this myself.

My head was spinning for the next several days, and sleep was almost impossible. I needed to get my worry and anxiety under control. I prayed a lot. I was confused... dazed... stunned. My emotions were everywhere. Bottom line, I was frightened. I was scared to death! I talked to my closest friends about what we had discovered. Nobody seemed very worried about it. She's a good kid—an athlete—never been in trouble, has a job, always so friendly. She's okay, just making some dumb choices like so many teenagers do. The counseling should help, and she will surely grow out of this phase. I wanted to believe all of that. I convinced myself they were right.

Things slowly returned to normal around the house. Regan was always amiable, never combative, and at home (in her room) most of the time she wasn't at work or practice. She really was fun to be around when she wasn't asleep. As promised, we got her a dog off Craigslist—a little twelve-pound Maltese mix named Sofi. She was about two years old, house-trained, full of fleas, and very smart. She bonded with Regan immediately, and once she was rid of the fleas, she had the run of the house. We all fell in love with her. Having Sofi really seemed to perk up Regan's mood.

She also started seeing a counselor. We were optimistic that we had caught this problem early and were taking proactive steps to fix it. I researched alternative high school options—she only had one year left. Did it really matter where she finished? It just mattered that she finished, right?

We drove to Siesta Key, Florida, from Texas at the end of July for Nationals. The three of us in a car for sixteen hours each way wasn't bad at all. The weather didn't cooperate fully for the tournament, but the beach was beautiful, and the girls had some great matches, and we all got plenty of sun and fun! When the girls wanted some alone time to explore the beach and the area, I got very nervous but let them go and have fun. They took some really pretty pictures and got ice cream, which totally didn't seem like what a drug user would do with her free time, so I relaxed some. She was still my sweet girl. It was a fun trip for us all.

Regan saw the counselor a few times, but then headed to Arizona in mid-August to spend a week-long visit with her dad before school started. It was clear how much she loved Sofi when she coerced her dad into purchasing an additional plane ticket to bring her along. She was excited to go and really loved Arizona. She posted some really pretty pictures (on her Instagram) of her time there in Sedona and at the Grand Canyon. Any signs of drugs were non-existent, and when she came home, she told me she didn't think she needed to see the counselor anymore. I thought that meant progress, so I didn't push the issue. School was starting in just a few days, and life was about to get busy again. She was still working her hostess job, too, so scheduling would've been difficult, but not impossible. I felt like the best thing was to let it go and hope for the best.

She'd decided to finish her senior year back at Magnolia West instead of at a different school. It all seemed like a sign that things were going back to normal—that the drug thing was just a phase, and she was moving on from it. I felt some relief and could relax a little more.

Hurricane Harvey hit Houston at the end of August, right when school was supposed to start. Instead of getting back into a routine, we found ourselves trapped inside while the sky dumped an ocean's worth of water on us. For days, it rained buckets *nonstop*. We were lucky—our house stayed dry, and we never lost power.

So naturally, we did what any responsible, flood-surviving family would do: binge-watched TV, plowed through a ridiculous amount of junk food, and stared out the window in disbelief as the water kept rising. Poor Sofi was the most miserable of us all—her disdain for the rain was unmatched, and every trip outside was met with utter disgust.

In the aftermath, some close friends of ours weren't as lucky. Their house flooded, and they needed a place to stay while making repairs. We had extra room, so they, along with their twenty-two-year-old son, moved in with us for a couple of months. Now, sharing your home and personal space with another family is always *an adventure.* But we got along fine—no major catastrophes, just the occasional *Can I ever walk around my own house in pajamas again?* moment. Regan didn't have friends over since our space was limited, but she didn't really complain. She was busy with school and work and mostly kept to herself.

Early on in our houseguests' stay, they mentioned that their son had something called Irlen Syndrome—a learning impairment that affects how the brain processes visual information. As they rattled off his symptoms—sensitivity to light, frequent migraines, fatigue, difficulty concentrating, words on a page appearing blurry or moving, poor depth perception—I felt a weird sense of déjà vu.

Hold on. *Regan has all of those things.* For *years,* she had complained about these exact struggles, but we had chalked it up to needing glasses (which she didn't), being overtired, or, let's be honest, teenage exaggeration. Turns out, Irlen Syndrome was *very real*—and we had never even heard of it.

Wasting no time, I scheduled an assessment for Regan just after her seventeenth birthday. The results? She was diagnosed as a *severe* case. The solution? Tinted lenses—custom-colored to calm her brain and stop the words on the page from doing the cha-cha. This information was life-changing. For years, she had struggled in school, convinced she just wasn't smart enough. She had fought through assignments, battled self-doubt, and unknowingly pushed herself through a condition that had nothing to do with her intelligence. The impact on her self-esteem had been brutal. But now, we had answers. Everything was going to be *so* much better now! She just needed to wear these colored glasses, and all of her school struggles would disappear! College would actually be an option now! *Hallelujah!*

I wish that had been the case. While she initially was relieved to find out there was a reason for her struggles, she quickly rejected the notion of wearing her colored glasses in school. She did not want to stand out, and she did not want anyone to think there was something wrong with her. Kids can be mean, and she'd already experienced enough of that. This was just one more thing that made her feel like she didn't fit in. At seventeen, the damage to her self-esteem had already been done.

In September, she decided she was quitting volleyball. My heart sank having that conversation with her. She had so much potential and loved the sport so much. Not to mention how many wonderful friends we'd made and the fun trips we'd taken over the years to watch her play. It seemed such a shame that she would quit playing during her last year of high school. We talked about whether she would regret her decision later on and what her reasons were for not wanting to continue playing. She just said she didn't want to play anymore. I couldn't force her to, so that was that. It was her choice, even if it disappointed me. I tried hard to separate what I wanted for her from what she wanted for herself, but I still really hated that decision and hoped she'd eventually miss it and want to return to playing.

Regan seemed to be more into her senior year in high school than I expected. She hadn't wanted a class ring when the school was selling them the prior year, and after insisting in July that she never wanted to go back to West, she surprised me when she wanted to make her own "senior overalls" for the Homecoming football game. This is a tradition that I was not familiar with, even after twenty-five years of living in Texas. We did not do half of the traditions in Iowa, where I grew up, that they do here in Texas! She refused to attend the homecoming dance, but she made and wore her own overalls, which were really cute. I helped her with them, but she designed them and picked out all the fabric and decorations. She was adamant that the homecoming dance was lame and more fun for the underclassmen than for the seniors, and she had no interest in going. I felt a little robbed at not getting to shop for her last fancy homecoming dress and watch her get all dolled up for pictures and a fun night with friends, but arguing with her would have served no purpose. I let it go and let it be her decision, and then tried to look at the positives, like all the money I'd saved by not having to buy a dress, shoes, make-up, hair, dinner, etc.

Every fall, from late September until almost Thanksgiving, the Renaissance Festival takes over Todd Mission, Texas—just six miles north of Magnolia. It lasts eight weekends and causes all kinds of traffic problems in our little town. However, they hire a lot of workers, and most of the vendors there pay pretty well, so Regan and a few of her friends went out there and got jobs for the duration of the 2017 festival. She worked in a photo booth near the entrance, helping dress customers in elaborate costumes for their portraits. The long weekend shifts would be tiring, but we were optimistic she'd earn and save a good amount of money.

On top of her RenFest job, she continued working at the restaurant, making her schedule even busier. Unfortunately, the aftermath of Hurricane Harvey impacted festival attendance, and as a result, she didn't get as many hours as expected. Still, what unsettled me the most wasn't how much she was making—but how she never seemed to have any money.

Her financial responsibilities were minimal: gas and $100 toward her car insurance each month. Yet, she struggled to cover even that. By October, I wasn't sure she was paying it at all. I questioned her repeatedly, trying to understand where her money was going, but her answers were vague. What stood out most was how often she withdrew cash from the ATM. Since I was linked to her bank account, I could see her transactions, though I rarely checked. But when I did, I didn't like what I saw. Something wasn't adding up. I suspected she was cashing her paychecks instead of depositing them, but I had no way of proving it. I couldn't determine how much money should have been there without knowing how many hours she was working, but I knew there should have been more than nothing.

She always changed her clothes before coming home from work, which I thought was odd. This was another reason that I was never sure how many hours she was actually at work. I'd ask, and she always gave me a plausible reason or excuse. Sometimes, she said she hadn't liked wearing her costume from the day—it was hot, sweaty, and uncomfortable by the end of her shift. Sometimes, she went and did something after work and didn't want to have work clothes on. Most of her clothes seemed to be kept in her car anyway... she's always had clothes everywhere, so that wasn't unusual. Aggravating for me as her mom, but not unusual.

It was now well into October, and things were going alright. She changed her mind about volleyball and went back out to the sand courts for some practice and to see her friends. She was excited once again to play and said she had really missed it. I was thrilled at this but tried to play it cool, keeping in mind that this was her decision, not mine, and wanting it to be just that—HERS. I truly thought at this point that we were in the clear. She was participating in school to a degree, back in the sand, had her Irlen diagnosis and a workable solution, and was working two jobs. I was pretty sure she wasn't using drugs anymore. Looking back, I ignored the negatives and focused solely on the positives.

On October 28th, 2017, Tim and I arrived around 7 p.m. at a Halloween costume party at a friend's home nearby in Magnolia. This was a party we'd attended for several years and always looked forward to. I was dressed in a royal blue *I Dream of Jeannie* genie costume, and Tim was a pilot. About an hour after we'd arrived, my phone rang. It was Regan. She was working at the RenFest that day, and I'd told her we would be at this party that evening, so it was very odd for her to be calling me. I didn't think too much of it—maybe she'd forgotten—and I answered, "Hello?"

"Mom, I've been in a car accident, and they are asking me if I should go to the hospital. Should I let them take me to the hospital?"

"What? Are you hurt? What happened? Who is asking you if you want to go to the hospital?" Despite the music playing, our friends stopped chatting and turned to focus on me.

"I'm in the ambulance, and they are asking if I want them to take me to the hospital. They told me to call you and ask you. Some lady hit me when I was turning left at the light on Butera to go home. What should I do?"

"Are you hurt? Do you think you need to go to the hospital?" I looked at Tim for support. His face displayed both confusion and concern. He said, "We can go now."

"I don't know. I think I passed out. My head hurts, and my

wrist hurts."

"Go to the hospital. We will meet you there. Ask if they are taking you to Tomball."

"Okay. Yes, Tomball. I love you, Mom."

"I love you, too. See you in a few minutes."

Panic sets in. Even when you know your child is physically alright, you can't help but freak out a little bit at the thought of what might have been. We left the party in our costumes and headed straight to the hospital. Thankfully, I had brought a matching cape in case I got cold, and I wrapped it around myself, suddenly self-conscious about walking into an emergency room in full costume. We arrived just minutes before they wheeled her in on a stretcher. She was alright but dazed, tired, and getting more sore as time passed. They ran all sorts of tests on her and determined she had a sprained wrist, bruised knee, and a concussion. We got to take her home after a few hours. Her Honda Accord, which she loved, was totaled, but she was okay, and we were thankful the officer who came to the scene did not write her a ticket. She is adamant the accident wasn't her fault, but there was no way to prove either way. We only had liability insurance on her car. Bummer.

I honestly did not ask Regan, and I'm not even sure it crossed my mind that she may not have been clean when she had her car accident. There was no blood drawn or any suspicion of anything like that by either the police or the doctors at the hospital. I really thought we were through with the drug phase. I think Tim had his suspicions, but he never said anything. If he did, I discounted it. My focus was on being thankful that she was alive and going to be healed up after a few days' rest. Sunday night, I resisted the urge to crawl into bed with her and just hold her while I cried. I almost lost her. I could have lost her. The thought sent a shudder through me, and tears fell down my cheeks. Relief and terror twisted together inside me, making it hard to breathe. My sweet, sweet girl.

She briefly returned to volleyball practice, but her headaches from the concussion limited her playing time. She lost interest in playing again within just a couple of weeks, but also, the weather started to cool off enough that practices were canceled, or there was a break between the fall and winter sessions—I can't remember which (maybe a little of both). The timing was coincidental enough that we didn't really talk about it. Whether she wanted to practice or not wasn't an issue because there weren't any practices to go to during that time.

One night in particular, just a couple of weeks after her accident, Regan had gone out with friends. It was a Saturday. She either had the day off from work at the RenFest or was off early that day. She took advantage of the time and said she was meeting some friends at the lake in a nearby subdivision. This was a place she had hung out on multiple occasions, and the lake itself isn't all that big. The friends she said she was meeting were all girls I knew, so I didn't think much of it. She called me around 8 p.m. to say that she was having a good time, and she sounded happy. She was going to Tomball to see some other friends and would be home in a couple of hours. Her curfew was midnight. I remember feeling relieved that she was having a good time and even thought to call me.

Tim was getting ready for bed around 11 p.m., and I was waiting up for her. It was always hard for me to go to bed and go to sleep when my kids weren't home at night. I'd worry about their safety until I knew they were home, despite doing my best to relax. When the door opened just before midnight, I got up off the couch. However, what I witnessed was disturbing. Regan was being helped inside and to her room by her friend, Sara, and a boy I'd never seen before. She looked very out of it and just collapsed on her bed. She could barely open her eyes and barely speak, except to say that she'd eaten some pizza and gotten violently ill and thrown up several times. She just wanted to go to sleep. I asked her friends what she'd had to drink. They looked at me like they had no idea what I'd even said. Tim came out of the living room to look at the scene, and I could tell by the look on his face that he was concerned and very suspicious. The friends left quickly. I went to Regan's bed and tried to talk to her. She wanted me to leave her alone. I tried helping her take her clothes off to get more comfortable, but she resisted. I tried looking at her eyes, but she wouldn't open them for me. I pulled at her eyelids to see if I could tell anything. Were they red? Tim kept asking me that, but I couldn't really tell anything. They looked a little red, but not overly. How red was too red? Maybe she was just tired?

I also could not smell anything. I sniffed her hair, her clothes, her purse, the air, everything I could. Nothing. She lay on her bed while I dumped out her purse. She was conscious but did not make any attempts to stop me. I threw away a vape cartridge that she said was her friend's when I asked her what it was. There wasn't anything else in there that looked like it shouldn't be there. I was so torn. I was mad at her, but could not find any reason to be. Maybe she really was just sick from bad pizza. Could that be? She insisted that was all that was wrong and just wanted to go to sleep. I went to bed and got up at least two more times to go check on her, smell her, and try to look at her eyes again. I needed something to confirm Tim's suspicions or to prove that she was telling the truth, and this was not something more serious.

I finally resigned myself to go to bed and leave her to rest. She was scheduled to work the next day, so she would need to see how she felt early enough to call in sick if she wasn't better. And there was nothing else I could do for her or for myself. She'd never ever come home sick like this before. I was really in disbelief about the whole thing. She got up on Sunday morning and said she felt much better. She looked better to me, too. So she got herself ready for work and left, saying she loved me and would come home if she started feeling bad again. And that was that. Just some bad pizza. She was fine. I was so thankful.

REGAN

I only remember bits and pieces of that conversation on the porch. I was crying. I told them I was really depressed, and I asked for a dog to help me feel better. I don't even remember if I mentioned counseling, but I was fine with that, too—especially if it meant I could have a dog.

I don't remember how many times I saw the counselor, but I mostly remember parts of our first session. Right away, I realized she wasn't going to be helpful. I tried to tell her about all of our family stuff, and she responded with something about her sons—something completely unrelated to what I had just said. I remember sitting there, thinking, *I really don't care about your sons. I don't care.* At the end of that session, she asked me, "So are we not gonna do drugs anymore?" in this casual, almost dismissive way. I said, "Sure." That was when I knew for sure she didn't care or understand anything I had told her. I left there angry and determined to test her.

I still wanted to use, so the next time I went, I got high before I got there. She had no clue. I don't remember anything about that visit. Same with the third—and last—session. The only thing I remember about that one was that before I went, I pierced my second earring holes myself with a safety pin. After that, I told my mom I didn't need to go back.

When I asked for a dog and said I wouldn't do drugs anymore,

I wasn't completely truthful. I did really want a dog, and I thought it would help me not feel so sad and alone. When we went to see Sofi, and I got to hold her, I knew right away—she was mine. We made a pact right then and there that she would be with me forever.

As soon as we got home, I gave her a bath to get rid of the fleas, and that night, she slept in my room with me. She was perfect. But as great as having Sofi was, it didn't take away all my pain, and it didn't make me want to stop using drugs. By that point, drugs were already the only thing that made me happy.

But Sofi was the only thing that I really felt *loved* me. She became the reason that when I wasn't high, I wasn't suicidal—because I *couldn't* leave her. If I had Sofi, then I had to keep living. And since I had to keep living, I had to keep doing drugs because that kept me happy. I had so many thoughts about wanting to die, but I don't think I ever truly had the guts to do it. Maybe I didn't actually *want* to die. Sofi gave me a reason to stay. But at the same time, having to stay *hurt*, so drugs gave me the option to live *without* the hurt.

Going to Nationals in Florida is one of the few times I remember feeling okay—probably because I didn't use drugs at all during that trip. It was fun. It felt like an escape from my real life. My teammate was someone I liked, and she was more on the normal side of experimenting—so the most we did was vape nicotine. That was it.

I didn't *need* to use, because for once, my life just didn't feel real. I wasn't home. I wasn't in school. I wasn't stuck in my routine. I was just *there*, living in the moment. And that felt really, really good.

I had a similar experience when I visited my dad in Arizona. It was another break from reality, and I didn't care to use then, either.

Having Sofi there made it even better. I got to see my cousins. My dad and I rarely spent time alone, but the visit wasn't bad. It was just a nice pause before going back to everything I wanted to escape from.

Getting tested for Irlen Syndrome is kind of a blur. I remember being asked to read things and describe what the letters were doing. The colored overlays she gave me *did* help. For the first time, I realized why I had struggled in school for so long. It was weirdly validating—like, *Oh, so I'm not just stupid.*

I had always hated getting called on to read in class. Everyone else could just *read*, and when it was my turn, I would trip over the words. It took me forever. I'd try to read fast so people wouldn't think I was dumb, but that only made it worse.

The glasses helped. But wearing them? That was a different story. People stared. They asked questions. "Why are you wearing sunglasses inside?" I already hated my life—I wasn't about to make it worse by drawing even more attention to myself.

At the beginning of my senior year, I met Sara. She worked at the same restaurant I did. I think she had graduated the year before, but we became work buddies. One night, she casually mentioned smoking, and I told her I did, too. That was it—that was all it took. She asked if I wanted to smoke sometime with her, and of course, I did.

I liked Sara. Unlike the people I'd been hanging around with, she never used me for a ride or anything else. With my other "friends," I had started noticing that they only wanted to hang out when they *needed* something. I was just their transportation. That realization hurt, so I stopped dealing with them.

But Sara? She was different. She never judged me. She actually *checked in* on me. She wanted to see me, wanted to know how I was doing. And we had this *thing* we did together—this thing that made me happy, that changed my life, that *saved* my life. I finally had a *best friend*. To me, it felt really genuine. I felt really appreciated and loved.

As homecoming approached, I was feeling a little better. I had Sara now, and for the first time in a while, I didn't feel completely alone. I was excited to make my homecoming overalls—because that was the thing to do as a senior. I spent time decorating them, making them personal, making them *mine*.

But the excitement faded fast.

The second I got to school wearing them, I felt *stupid*. I looked around and saw all these other girls in their overalls, laughing and taking pictures with their best friends, making memories they'd keep forever. And me? I had no one. The only pictures I ended up in were either out of pity or because it was a *group* thing. It was just another reminder that I didn't belong.

Working at RenFest was pretty decent. Most of the money I made, I cashed out—because that was the only way to buy drugs. I always had something on hand for the right moment, and I'd stock up for things like my birthday. I worked there with the same group of friends I had been using with at school, at least before things started going south with them. Having a job together made it easy for us to hang out and get high before and after our shifts.

But I was the only one working the night I got in my wreck. None of those friends were there that day, so I hadn't used. I worked my full shift and was walking back to my car alone when some strange guy stopped me, asking if I wanted to go party with him. I told him, "No, I'm okay. You go have fun." But as I kept walking, I got paranoid. What if he followed me? What if he tried to kill me? I picked up my pace, got to my car, and drove off.

It still blows my mind that I wasn't high when I crashed that night. I was high pretty much every other day. I don't know if you'd call that a God moment or not, but somehow, that night, I really wasn't.

The thing about volleyball was that when I first quit, I was really struggling. But then I became friends with Sara, and even though things were technically worse, they *felt* better. I was using so much more, which meant I was happy all the time—at least in my mind—and I finally had a real friend. So, in a way, I was feeling good.

I missed volleyball, but by then, the weather had turned cold, and practices had ended. I never hated it. I actually loved it—loved the sport, loved the girls—but it became conflicting. At that point, it wasn't really about volleyball anymore. It was about the fact that it took time away from me using drugs, and drugs were the only thing that made me feel happy.

And as much as I loved the girls on my team and how nice they were to me, we all went our separate ways once practice ended. It never felt like a *real* connection. With Sara, though, I felt like I had finally found everything I had been looking for in one person. And obviously, I'm very codependent, too. It just made sense—why would I want to do anything *except* drugs? They were the only thing that made me happy, and now I had someone to do them with.

I don't remember much about the night I supposedly threw up pizza. I remember being with Sara and a bunch of people, and I know I took a lot of Xanax. I don't even know if I was drinking, too, but I *definitely* did a lot of Xanax.

At some point, I opened my eyes, and I was sitting in a living room. The next time I came to, Sara was sitting next to me, and

I was lying on a bed. Then I blacked out again. The next thing I remember, I was in the passenger seat of my car with Sara driving. There was a trash bag in my lap, and I guess I had been throwing up. I assume our other friend was following us so she'd have a ride back, but I don't really know. I blacked out again.

The last thing I remember was being in my bed, my mom hovering over me. After that? Nothing. Just darkness. But I know one thing for sure—it was definitely drugs.

In the beginning, and I know this sounds horrible, but using drugs felt like a *good* thing. I had zero ways of understanding my emotions or coping with the things I had been through. I just hated myself so much. It made me not want to live.

Even before drugs, when I was little, I would cry myself to sleep almost every night. I remember lying in bed after saying goodnight, sobbing into my pillow, *begging* God to just kill me. I didn't want to wake up and do it all over again the next day.

So when drugs came into the picture, it genuinely felt like they saved my life. If they had never been an option for me, I honestly believe I would have started self-harming or even attempted suicide. Drugs didn't fix anything, but they made it bearable. They took all the pain and darkness inside me and just *shut it off*. I didn't have to feel anything I didn't want to feel.

I really got to a point where I didn't understand why my mom thought it was such a big deal. In my mind, I wasn't doing something destructive—I was just trying to be happy. *Why was that a bad thing?*

Chapter 4
The Holidays

Thanksgiving came soon after, and we invited Regan's friend, Sara, to join us for the celebration at our friend's home in Rosenberg. These were the same wonderful friends we had spent that infamous 4th of July weekend with. Sara had needed a place to stay just prior to the holiday, and Regan had asked us if she could stay with us for a while, just until she could get back on her feet. She was her co-worker at the Mexican restaurant, and they became friends. Now that our other friends had moved back into their own home after Hurricane Harvey had displaced them, we had extra room. I agreed to let her stay temporarily. After all, no young girl should be out on the streets alone. I asked Regan why she didn't live with her own family, and she said she didn't really know, but her dad was really sick, and there were some issues going on with that. It was a very muddy explanation, but she had nowhere to stay, so in that moment, I felt compelled to meet that need.

The details I knew about Sara were sketchy at best. She was a year or so older than Regan, and her family didn't live too far away from us. She had worked at the Mexican restaurant with Regan, where they'd met and become friends. Since the Mexican restaurant had closed in October, she'd been looking for a job but had no transportation as her truck needed to be fixed. Her dad was supposed to help her fix her truck, but he was sick, so that was taking a lot longer than anticipated. She was going to beauty school in Tomball and relied on friends to get her where she needed to be, including Regan. And that was the extent of it.

So, of course, Sara would accompany us to our friends' home on Thanksgiving Day. Our friends were welcoming and happy to have us all. The girls dressed up and looked really nice for the day—make-up and everything. I thought they really had gone all out, but I was so happy because Regan hadn't fixed herself up that well in quite some time. How long had it been? I wasn't sure. I was just happy to see her look so good. I took a lot of pictures of her that day.

Our Thanksgiving tradition was simple but special—mimosas in hand, we cooked, chatted, and caught up on life. It felt warm, familiar, and joyful—the kind of day that made me grateful for the people around me. Regan and Sara joined in, sipping on mimosas alongside us. We kept their glasses limited, but it felt harmless—after all, it was a holiday, and we weren't going anywhere anytime soon. The house was filled with laughter, the scent of turkey and spices, and the occasional squeals of delight as we passed around our friends' new grandbaby. Even Sofi trotted happily from room to room, taking in all the love and attention. It was a good day.

After dinner, we played games around the table, still basking in the warmth of the evening. That's when I noticed it. Regan slumped in her chair, her eyelids heavy, barely keeping up with the dice game. At first, I brushed it off—the champagne probably made her sleepy, I reasoned. But something didn't sit right. My stomach churned as I watched her struggle to focus, to stay present. When the game ended, she didn't hesitate to curl up on the couch, eyes fluttering closed almost immediately.

Nobody else seemed to notice. Or maybe they did and didn't think anything of it. I tried to do the same—tried to convince myself it was nothing, that I was overthinking. We'd be heading home soon anyway. Still, I couldn't shake the unease creeping into my chest, a whisper in the back of my mind that I wasn't ready to listen to. And yet, despite the nagging worry, I decided I liked Sara. She was sweet, fun, and seemed to really like being with everyone.

We got home by 10 p.m. and were all tired, so we didn't stay up long. I woke up at some point in the middle of the night to Sofi barking. I saw a faint light through the cracks in our closed bedroom door, so I got up to see what was going on. Everything was blurry because I didn't have my contacts in, and I'm blind as a bat without them, but I wasn't concerned, just curious. I saw the light on in Regan's room across the house, but when I went in through the open door, it was empty. No Sofi either. Hmmm. I called Regan's name but got no answer. I didn't hear or see anything, so I assumed they were all upstairs where Sara was sleeping. Just girls staying up late chatting. It was Thanksgiving break. I went back to bed and back to sleep.

When I asked Regan why Sofi had been barking during the night, she seemed surprised, almost caught off guard. "Oh, we just went outside for a walk," she said casually as if it were the most natural thing in the world.

I hesitated; something about it not sitting quite right with me. The light had been on in her room, but when I checked, they were nowhere to be found. Sofi's barking had pulled me from sleep, and I had lain there for a while afterward, restless, unsettled. A walk? At that hour? Logically, it wasn't a big deal. It wasn't cold outside, and we lived in a quiet neighborhood tucked away where people didn't just happen upon us by accident. It wasn't unsafe. Still, something about it gnawed at me. Both girls were up and going the next morning, and there were no signs of anything unusual. I let it go.

I always did all the laundry at home. Regan was not tasked with much in the way of chores around the house. She was working, had school, and had been playing volleyball multiple times a week, so she didn't have a lot of time for chores. She did have to clean her room when it got really bad, and she would. When I did the laundry, I had lots of opportunities to check her clothing, which I did. I smelled everything. I checked pockets. I could not find anything suspicious. I tried to relax, but there was a nagging feeling I tried hard to ignore.

Her clothes started to change slowly—baggy shirts, darker colors. At first, I didn't really notice. But gradually, she started looking less like herself, her outfits resembling something a homeless person might wear. I would joke with her about it, teasing, "Why do you have to look like a homeless person?" She'd roll her eyes and chuckle, "Oh, Mom! This is comfortable." She said it so casually that I let it go, but I hated those all-black, oversized clothes. They swallowed her tiny one-hundred-and-five-pound frame, making her disappear inside them. Was this just a teenage phase? A fashion trend I was too old to understand?

She also stopped combing her hair every day. This might sound strange, but her hair was very long and hit her waist, so she would put it up on her head in a messy bun a lot. It tangled easily, and we have very hot weather in Texas, so she was in the habit of putting it up and leaving it there most of the time. She rarely wore it down by this time, though. Very rarely. And the weather was getting cooler. She would complain a lot about how annoying her hair was, but never wanted to cut it. I think it became a love-hate relationship. And while this annoyed me because I loved her hair down, I realized that it wasn't my hair—it was hers, and she could do with it what she wished.

Regan landed a job working at the retail store Five Below in Tomball around mid-November. Tomball was only about fifteen to twenty minutes away, and she would be working there as holiday help. They were generous with her hours, and she said she really liked the job, but the store manager was not nice. She had a bad habit of yelling at employees in front of customers and berating them for making mistakes. The store stayed open until midnight, and Regan routinely closed the store and worked even later. There were several nights toward Christmas that she would come home between 1:00 and 2:00 a.m. and then have to go to school the next morning. I never got up to greet her when she came home on any of those occasions. I wish I had. Normally, though, I'd call her, and she would answer after the store closed, that she was straightening things and would be home after that, or that she was walking to her car. I never suspected anything was off about that. I still don't know if she was telling the truth or not, I guess. I just thought she was getting a lot of hours and should be making decent money. We talked several times about her asking if they would keep her on after the holidays were over, as she wanted to stay there rather than find another job. I think they liked her enough to keep her part-time. This is where things kind of get fuzzy.

I scheduled a family photo session two weeks after Thanksgiving and two weeks before Christmas. It had been at least three years since we'd last taken professional pictures together, and with Regan graduating in just a few short months, I didn't want to let another year slip by. Who knew when we'd all be in the same place long enough to take another one?

Regan wanted to include Sofi in the photos. Tim protested—something about a dog not belonging in a family portrait—but there was no way I was going to tell her no. Sofi was hers, and that little dog had become such a significant part of her life. So, despite Tim's grumbling, we brought her along. The photographer indulged us, letting Sofi into some of the shots but not all.

The session itself was nice—surprisingly lighthearted. Regan looked beautiful in jeans and a red sweater, and I remember feeling so grateful that she was here with us, smiling for the camera. We planned to do her senior pictures in the spring, but I asked the photographer to snap a few solo shots since she was already dressed nicely. She wanted some with Sofi, and I figured, why not? I was already paying for the session and knew I'd want to hold onto as many memories of this time as possible.

The photographer sent us the preview a couple of days later, and I loved them. This was my Christmas present to myself, and I couldn't have been happier with how they turned out—except for my son's glaring absence. That stung, but I tried not to let it dampen the joy of finally having new pictures of our family.

When I got the final images in mid-January, I was more grateful than ever that I had insisted we take them. I had no idea at the time just how priceless they would become to me. But there was one photo of Regan—one I kept coming back to—that unsettled me. She wasn't smiling in it. Her expression wasn't sad, exactly, but her eyes… her eyes looked dark and empty. Surely, it was just some weird lighting.

I didn't mark it as a favorite, but I couldn't bring myself to ignore it, either. I found myself looking at it again and again, feeling something in my chest tighten each time. But I didn't dwell on it. Instead, I focused on the pictures where she was smiling and got busy choosing my favorites to frame.

Christmas is always a busy time. We were all working, and then there was the shopping, the planning, the parties, and the decorating. It's the time of year when we are all going ninety to nothing and in all different directions. This year, there was a Houston Texans football game on Christmas Day. That might not mean anything to most people, but we have owned season tickets to the Texans since 2002, so a home game on Christmas Day meant we were at NRG Stadium on Christmas. This was the first time that had happened, and I was not particularly happy about it. Since it was just us, we went and made the most of it. I bought an extra ticket so Regan could go with us, and we also planned to meet some friends and Tim's cousins at the game.

The Friday before Christmas, we hosted a holiday party at our home for several of our friends. It was meant to be casual—good food, drinks, a White Elephant gift exchange, and some fun games. Regan was on Christmas break from school, so I had one small request: that she would make her famous cake balls decorated to look like adorable little snowmen, just like the ones she had made for her nutrition class. I had been asking her all week, reminding her repeatedly that she needed to start early so they would be ready in time. She kept putting it off. "I'll get to it, Mom." Finally, there was no time left to procrastinate—the party was that night. The cake balls had to be made.

When I got home from work that afternoon, I expected to find beautifully decorated cake balls chilling in the fridge. Instead, I walked into the kitchen to find Regan and a friend (whom I had never met before) in full panic mode, scrambling to finish the cake balls. My eyes darted to the trays, and my heart sank. The snowmen were a disaster. They had run out of white candy coating, leaving the frosting thin and uneven. The cake balls were lumpy blobs and anything but round.

Regan had to get ready for work and leave by 4:00 p.m. to take her friend home and make it to work on time. It appeared as if they had started on the cake balls for the party around 2:30... giving themselves an hour and a half to make over thirty cake balls, decorate them, shower, and get ready for work. I was so disappointed. It would have been nice if the balls they made actually looked presentable!

As the girls hurried out the door, I stood frozen in the kitchen, staring at the trays of ruined cake balls. *This can't be happening.* With a deep sigh, I grabbed one and examined it. The coating was too thin, the shape uneven, and there was no way I was serving these at my party. Frustration bubbled up, but I had no choice—I was in full-on damage control mode. I peeled the coating off every single cake ball, rolled them back into something resembling a round shape, and then ran out the door to the grocery store, *praying* they had more candy coating. Of course, they didn't. I grabbed the next best thing and hoped for a Christmas miracle.

After what felt like hours of reconstructive cake ball surgery, I was able to salvage enough of the balls for the party, but only about twelve were the cute snowmen that I had envisioned. Oh well. Nobody at the party would know that they weren't what I'd asked for, and at least they tasted good.

I was still baffled, though. *Why, when she had literally the entire day free, had she waited until the last possible moment?* I could not come up with a reasonable answer, but Regan was already at work, and our guests would be arriving soon. No big deal. I didn't dwell on it once our friends arrived. The party was a lot of fun, and the cake balls were a mere inconvenience.

We always open Christmas presents on Christmas Eve. We

figured out how to set up FaceTime with my family at my sister's house in Iowa so that we could be together while opening the gifts we sent to each other. It worked out pretty well. Everyone took turns opening presents. Regan was given a new MacBook computer from us and her Uncle Howie. Since it was her senior year and she'd gotten the glasses to help with her Irlen Syndrome, we were excited at the prospect of her being able to attend college after high school. She would need a computer, and she had asked for one every year for several years. I was so excited to give it to her. I wrote out a card with it that said:

> *Your greatest challenge is your greatest gift.*
>
> *Regan,*
> *Merry Christmas to my beautiful, capable, smart, and loving daughter! Before you open this present, we wanted you to know the significance of it. This gift represents our belief in YOU… that you have the capability of doing BIG things with your life… and that you have nothing holding you back from your dreams anymore. Your Irlen Syndrome diagnosis has been a game-changer in so many ways. It is up to you to decide to use it as an excuse or as your motivation. Every single person on earth has trials and struggles in life… use them to make*

you stronger, more determined, and more kind and compassionate toward others.

This gift is meant to help you realize your goal of going to and graduating from college. A dream that will now become a reality. How blessed you are <3

WE BELIEVE IN YOU, REGAN! You will always have us in your corner cheering you on!!

Love,

Mom, Tim, and Uncle Howie

She cried when she read it and opened the computer. She was so surprised and excited! I was really happy for her. I think we all were. It was unusual for us to spend so much on a Christmas gift.

That evening, Regan spent hours carefully assembling a gingerbread house from a kit we had been given. The living room was quiet; the only sounds were the crinkle of plastic wrappers and the occasional clink of candy against the table. As I watched her work, so focused and meticulous, a familiar memory surfaced—her as a little girl, sitting cross-legged in the living room, completely absorbed in her Polly Pockets. She would spend hours dressing them up, swapping their tiny plastic clothes, shoes, and hats, creating stories for them as if the rest of the world didn't exist. She was like that now, lost in the simple joy of building something, piece by piece. For the first time in a long while, I felt a wave of hopefulness wash over me. Maybe, just maybe, she was finding her way back to herself.

We got up on Christmas morning and got dressed in our Texans gear—Regan borrowed a shirt from me as she wasn't much of a football fan. She really wasn't much of a fan of any sport, and she wasn't thrilled to have to go to an NFL game, but I was glad she was willing to dress the part and make the most of it. We tailgated for a couple of hours before the game. Tailgating consisted of sitting in the parking lot in chairs and having some drinks and food while leisurely chatting and enjoying the atmosphere. The weather wasn't bad—it was cool, but we had blankets, long sleeves, and coats if we needed them. We let Regan have a drink in the parking lot with us. I think it was some kind of root beer with alcohol in it. She sipped it, and we thought nothing of it. I am not sure whether she had one or two during the couple of hours we sat out there, but we also ate some snacks Tim had prepared for us. It was a lighthearted time, and a guy I knew from work had brought his son to the game—they were Steelers fans and joined us in the parking lot as well. His son was in his early twenties, and Regan was seventeen, but being the youngest in our small crowd, they started chatting naturally.

During the football game, in which the Steelers soundly crushed our Texans, we all had a great time. Regan actually enjoyed watching the action and wished she had come to a game sooner. As a football fan, I loved that she was loving it so much! We got home later that evening, having all decided it was a pretty awesome Christmas Day—not what we were used to, but really fun anyway. It is hard to believe that our lives would be flipped upside down and inside out just one week later.

REGAN

At this point, I really can't tell you much about what was going on other than a lot of drugs. My memory from that time is vague, and honestly, I feel like the only reason I even remember some things is because of photos. There are only a few experiences that I genuinely recall.

Thanksgiving started with Sara hanging out, playing with the baby, and having Sofi with us. At some point, Sara and I ate something edible—a Rice Krispies treat with M&Ms in it. After that, I was high, so I don't remember much of the rest of the day.

Sometime over Thanksgiving break, I remember being upstairs, and I know at some point we smoked. I don't think we smoked at the house, though. I think we had gone out, smoked somewhere else, and then came back late. Once we were upstairs, we did ecstasy. Another night, I remember sneaking out through my bedroom window, but Sofi didn't come with us. Some other friends picked us up down the street, and we left with them to smoke. I have no idea how long we were gone.

Working at Five Below, there were plenty of times I'd get off work, stop by to see Sara, and get high. But there were also nights when I had the late restocking shift. That's when the store would get all their shipments in, and my job was to fold shirts and put away the new merchandise. If I had a late shift, I'd always get high before work. I really couldn't have cared less about folding shirts. But there were a few times when I'd do Molly or cocaine before my shift, and suddenly, I was having the time of my life folding those shirts. I'd put my headphones in—no customers, no coworkers to deal with—just me, my music, and my own little world. Now, apparently, I couldn't make cake balls while I was high, so I don't know what those folded shirts actually looked like, but I had fun doing it.

I don't remember opening any gifts at Christmas, but that doesn't necessarily mean I got high right before. I just don't remember. The drugs were definitely doing damage to my brain. I think any drug addict will tell you that their memory is terrible because of the damage it does. I seem to remember more of the experiences when I was high rather than when I wasn't. Maybe it's because, at that time, getting high was the only thing that made me feel good. Those moments felt like pure happiness, like relief, so they stuck with me more. I don't remember watching the Texans game on Christmas Day, but I know I had a good time. I faintly recall a mascot—I think I took a picture with it or something.

Looking back at photos from that time, I can piece together certain things. I know I got my new car on November 3rd. It wasn't actually new, but it was new to me—a medium blue 2008 Honda Element. November 10th was the first time I did cocaine, and the next day was the first time I did Molly. Most of my photos from that time just remind me of the drugs I was doing that day. There's a photo of me getting my computer for Christmas, but I don't remember that at all. My life was a literal blur. I was getting high before school, leaving school to get high, and using every night—sometimes multiple times.

By Christmas, my drug use was out of control. I was using all the time, every day. I was skipping certain class periods, and since Mom and Tim were at work, I'd come home to smoke. Sometimes, I'd go back to school, and sometimes, I wouldn't. Instead, I'd go see Sara. At first, I was only skipping one class and coming back, but then I started wondering why I was even bothering to come back at all. So I just stopped. I had no friends at school—what was the point?

I met Taylor through Sara. For a short time, the three of us hung out together, but then Sara kind of vanished. It was weird—she just wasn't around anymore. I think she ended up getting involved with some really sketchy people, stripping for money, and who knows what else. Without Sara, Taylor and I bonded over worrying about her. We used together, and at first, I was probably using her for her drugs because she always had some. But after Sara hurt my feelings by disappearing from my life, Taylor and I actually became friends.

There was one time when our whole group was hanging out, and Sara barged in in a hurry. She was different—off—like she wasn't even herself. She didn't acknowledge any of us, and then, just as fast as she appeared, she was gone again. That was the last time I saw her. After that, Taylor and I started hanging out alone. I had a car, so I'd give her rides a lot. I never really considered her my best friend, but she was the person I spent the most time with. And at that point, I didn't have anyone else.

Chapter 5
Kicked Out

The next couple of days passed quietly, a calm before the storm I didn't yet see coming. Tim and I were finalizing our New Year's Eve plans while also preparing for our anniversary trip to Austin that weekend. Meanwhile, Regan was set to fly to Phoenix, Arizona, on New Year's Day to visit her dad for a week before starting the final semester of her senior year. Everything felt normal—until Thursday evening, when Regan asked if she could spend the night at her friend Taylor's house. Taylor was the same friend who had "helped" with the cake ball snowman disaster, and something about the request made me uneasy. I couldn't quite put my finger on why, but my initial instinct was to say no. Regan, however, wasn't one to give up easily. She pleaded, layering in reasons, assurances, and even promises. "Please, Mom, I swear we'll have a day together this weekend—just the two of us!" Her enthusiasm was relentless, and despite the small voice in my head telling me to stand firm, I caved.

Still, I set clear expectations. She needed to be home by 9 a.m. sharp because Tim and I were heading to Austin later that morning. Our anniversary had been in November, but we had planned this trip weeks ago—a night in a hotel, just the two of us, and tickets to see the Kansas Jayhawks play the Texas Longhorns. It was our first time leaving Regan home alone overnight, and though I hesitated for a brief moment, I reassured myself—she was almost done with high school, and she had earned our trust. Before she left, I asked for the phone number of Taylor's parents, just in case I needed to check in. Regan handed it over without hesitation, something she had always done without complaint. Looking back, I don't even remember when she walked out the door that night. I was too caught up in my own excitement, checking off last-minute to-dos before our trip and imagining myself sitting in the stands, watching my favorite team play. At that moment, it never crossed my mind that I should have paid more attention.

I woke up early that morning, around 7:30, still feeling groggy but eager to start the day. I had a lot to do before Tim and I left for Austin, including getting the oil changed in my car—a task I had put off the day before. As 9:00 came and went, irritation prickled at me. Regan was supposed to be home. I grabbed my phone and texted her, keeping it short and direct: *You're late.* A few minutes later, she responded, saying Taylor's mother had made them break-fast and she would head home once they were finished eating. I exhaled slowly, trying to shake off my annoyance. *Okay,* I thought, *at least she's not ignoring me.* That was nice of Taylor's mom, I reasoned, and I texted back that it was fine. With that settled, I turned my attention back to getting myself ready for the day, feeling a little more at ease.

Around 10:00, I grabbed my purse and headed out. As I pulled up to the exit gate of our neighborhood, I saw Regan's car—a car I could recognize anywhere—driving past. My stomach twisted. *Wait a second.* Something wasn't right. She was heading in the *op-*

posite direction she should have been—back toward Taylor's. That didn't make any sense. My breath caught in my throat as the realization hit: she had lied to me. The frustration I had been holding at bay surged forward. Without thinking, I grabbed my phone and called her, my heart pounding as I pressed it to my ear. The moment she picked up, I skipped the pleasantries.

"Why are you going the opposite way you should be going?" My voice was sharper than I intended, but I didn't care. There was a slight pause before she answered, her voice too casual, too rehearsed.

"Oh, um… we ran out of milk for breakfast, so I had to go get some."

I tightened my grip on the steering wheel, my knuckles turning white. "Really? *Where* did you go to get milk?"

"The Shell station," she answered quickly.

Wrong answer. My pulse hammered in my ears as my frustration boiled over. "Why didn't you go to the Exxon or the Dollar Store? They're *a lot* closer to Taylor's house." I could feel the heat rising in my chest, my gut screaming at me that something was very, very wrong. This wasn't just a small, harmless lie. This was deliberate. Calculated. And I wasn't about to let it slide.

She was fumbling for an explanation by this time, and we were almost to Taylor's house. I was hot on her tail. The milk they needed was special or something. I don't know. Whatever she said, I knew was a lie. I pulled into Taylor's parents' driveway behind them, and I was furious. I blocked them in, got out of my car, and went to Regan's side. She put her window down as I yelled, "Where were you last night?" I probably yelled other things because she didn't give much of an answer. I don't know if she told me at that time that they'd slept in her car at a park in Tomball or if she told me that later.

I marched up to the front door as Taylor started gathering her things from Regan's car. Her mother answered the door and was instantly confused. Angrily and a bit too loudly, I told her I was Regan's mom, and then I asked, "Did the girls spend the night here last night?"

"No. They said they were spending the night at your house."

"Well, they told me they were spending the night here last night, and they were NOT at my house either."

At that point, there wasn't much else to say. I was angry, and they were caught. I still needed my oil changed. I walked back to Regan's car and told Taylor to get her crap and get out of her car. I told Regan to meet me at home. I was going to get my oil changed, and I would talk to her when I returned. It was probably a good thing I gave myself an hour or two to think and to calm down a bit. I hate liars. And my daughter was a liar.

When I got home, I went straight to Regan's room. I knew I would find her there. She was on her bed, just sitting there. I supposed she was waiting for me to dole out her punishment. I didn't say a whole lot. I started with, "If I drug-tested you right now, would you pass?"

She lifted her head to meet my stare and flatly said, "No." It felt like a knife to the heart. She wasn't trying to hide it. She wasn't making excuses. She was just… gone.

I swallowed hard and pressed on. "I told you before that you can't do drugs and live here. I can't have it around me. It's illegal."

She just stared at me. No anger. No sadness. No remorse. Just nothing. My little girl—the sweet, bright, joyful child I had raised—was a stranger to me now. A hollow shell of who she used to be.

I told her she had to stop using drugs. She said she wasn't going to stop. She said she didn't want to stop. She didn't say it angrily or even disrespectfully. She said it like it was fact… in a way that let me know she was serious and there was nothing I could do or say to change her mind. It wasn't up for discussion.

What I did next surprised us both. My thoughts were everywhere, but essentially, I knew that she meant what she said and that I could not live with it. I dialed her dad's phone number, hit the speakerphone button, and laid it down on her bed between us. He answered, which was actually a surprise since we hadn't spoken to each other in a very long time. "Hello?"

I told him in a very brief form that Regan had been caught using drugs last July, and then last night said she was spending the night with a friend, who told her mother they were spending the night with us, and then they were out all night somewhere. I said, "Regan said she wouldn't pass a drug test and that she didn't want to stop using drugs. So, on Monday, when she gets on the plane to come and visit you, she will not be coming back home."

He didn't have a chance to say much. I'm sure he was shocked and mostly trying to process it all in a matter of just a couple of minutes. He stuttered his "okay" but agreed that she would be coming there to stay. I hung up the phone. Regan just looked at me. She didn't say anything. Still no emotion. Nothing. I was in disbelief that this was happening and struggled to keep it together. My anger was melting into fear and overwhelming sadness.

I thanked her for ruining our anniversary trip that I had been so excited about, but we were going to go anyway. I instructed her to start packing her things so that she could take as much with her on the plane as possible, since we didn't know how long it would be before she could get the rest of it. Sofi could stay with us until arrangements could be made for her to go to Arizona. She might have said okay, but she might have said nothing. I don't remember. It wasn't a conversation. It was simply instructions and nothing else. My heart was breaking. *What have I done?*

I was in a fog now. Preparing to leave for the night, trying to talk to Tim about the situation, so many thoughts ran through my head: *Did I do the right thing? Why doesn't she want to stop using drugs? Will I ever see her again? Will getting her away from these friends help? What about school? How am I supposed to have fun now? Will she still be here when we get home tomorrow? Am I doing the right thing?* And the loop kept going incessantly.

We left shortly after my talk with her, and I was thankful for a two-hour drive to try to make sense of it all. Really, I spent that time trying to justify what I had done. I talked to Tim, who agreed with my decision, but that wasn't enough. Of course, he wanted her gone… he was the stepdad and didn't want to deal with this crap. I didn't blame him. I called my sister, Teresa. She'd had some issues for quite a few years growing up, so I thought she would be able to offer some advice. Her reaction to the news was shock, but she was also supportive. The biggest takeaway from our talk was that Regan's best chance for change was removing her from her current circle of friends/people. "Nothing will change if she stays where she is and with the same people," she said. I agree with that. You are who you surround yourself with. Everyone knows that. Okay. I started to feel a little better about my decision to send her away. My panic started to alleviate.

Next, I called my best friend. She'd dealt with drug issues with all three of her children in one capacity or another, so I knew I could talk to her. She was honest in saying that, without really knowing the extent of Regan's drug use, she could only offer me advice based on her own experience. She'd had to kick her daughter out about a year earlier for the same reason, so she completely understood what that felt like. Her daughter returned within a few months and had turned her life around, so she also offered that example as hope. She confirmed my boundary that using drugs was not okay and would not be tolerated in or near my home or my family, and that enforcing that was okay for me to do. I needed permission for that. It felt wrong and mean and ugly. I needed to hear that it was okay. I didn't fully embrace it yet, but it helped to hear someone tell me that I wasn't being a terrible mom. She also knew my history with Regan's dad and current situation with our son. Because of all of that, she asked if there wasn't somewhere else we could send her instead. We wrestled with that question because her point was valid. Would he turn her against me, too?

I couldn't send her to my mom's in Iowa. Drugs were rampant in her town, and she had often talked about that in conversations. My sister lived in another small town in Iowa and said they had the same issues with drugs—they were everywhere. Other than those two, there wasn't anyone else I would even consider. You can't just call up a family member you haven't talked to in a while and say, "Hey! Regan is having a hard time here, and we caught her using drugs for the second time in six months, so would you mind if she moved in with you so you can monitor her every move?" Nope. There wasn't anyone I could think of who would even begin to explore that situation with me. I had one choice and one choice only—her dad.

The tears finally came, hot and relentless, slipping down my face faster than I could wipe them away. There was nobody else I could talk to. Nobody else I even wanted to tell. This wasn't something I could share casually—it was a private, crushing weight pressing down on my chest, making it hard to breathe. I felt awful. Awful that this has cast a dark cloud over our anniversary trip. Awful that I couldn't just push it aside and enjoy myself. I had only two more days with her before she was leaving.

My head was just spinning. And my husband was trying his best to console me and salvage our anniversary trip. The game was starting in a few hours, and we'd paid good money for good seats. "There's nothing we can do until we get home. Please, let's try to have a little fun." I think he knew it was a long shot, but he also knew I would try.

There was no contact with Regan that night—no text messages and no phone calls. I figured she was doing whatever she wanted since we were not home, and I tried not to think about it. This would be her last hurrah, and there was nothing I could do about it.

We checked into our hotel, walked to a restaurant to eat dinner, and got to our seats at the Frank Erwin Center early so we could watch warm-ups. Even though I was crying off and on until the game started, I was actually able to enjoy the game itself. Basketball is so fast-paced and fun to watch, and the Jayhawks won—I was grateful for that. We knew where the team would exit the arena after the game, so we lined up outside, hoping to get pictures with the players before they boarded the bus back to Kansas. Surprisingly, we were able to get pictures with all of the players and even Coach Self. I'm amazed that I was smiling in all of them. My heart was still breaking inside.

I didn't sleep much at all that night. My mind would not quiet. I could not stop all of the scenarios that were playing in my head and all of the doubts about what was about to happen. Not to mention wondering where Regan was at that moment, what she was doing, and who she was with. So many thoughts. They kept me awake, and I cried a lot. I prayed, too. *Lord, please help me to know whether this is the right thing or not. Lord, please don't leave me—I don't think I can handle losing my daughter, too. Lord, please don't let her use drugs anymore. Lord, show me what you want me to do. I'm clinging to You with everything I've got left in me.*

Tim and I returned home the next day. The two-hour drive home was difficult for me because I didn't really want to go home, and I also knew I *needed* to get home. I wasn't sure what I would find when we got there or how I would get through the next forty-eight hours. My emotional state was all over the place: fearful, angry, sad, shocked, second-guessing my decision, and reliving that conversation on her bed over and over again. Halfway home, we passed an antique store, and I asked Tim to stop. I needed a little more time, but I'm not sure why. My heart was beating out of my chest.

When we got home, Regan was there, sitting in the living room with Sofi, watching TV. It was as if nothing had happened, but there was tension in the air. There was also a strong smell of marijuana in her room that we had to air out while Tim went outside to go through her car. He found pot inside, along with bedding and a host of perfumes and potpourri sprays. She received strict instructions to clean every inch of her car. I looked at her bank account, which we shared, but I had never made a habit of checking up on her. There were a large number of cash withdrawals that we presumed were used to purchase marijuana. I was not willing to make the assumption that the problem was anything other than pot.

She did pack quite a bit while we were gone, which made it seem like she was ready to leave. I reminded her that she needed to pack everything before she left so that when she came back to pick it up, it would be an easy process, adding that there had better not be any drugs in there. She didn't have anything to say, really, so at least there wasn't any arguing. She did as she was told. I confiscated her phone, brand new computer, and her car keys.

The following day was New Year's Eve, and we had already planned to attend a small party at a friend's home. There was always alcohol around, and we were regular social drinkers. I decided that Regan would have to go to the party with us because she needed supervision, obviously, and her flight was scheduled for the following morning. I couldn't risk her not being able to get on that plane. The three of us went to the party, and Tim and I did our best to act like our worlds hadn't just been turned upside down in the previous forty-eight hours. There was no way I was telling anyone what was going on.

Regan was polite and friendly, holding and entertaining a six-month-old baby much of the time. We shared at least one bottle of champagne throughout the evening while Tim drank shots with the guys. I struggled to mingle with our friends and keep my eye on my daughter at the same time. It felt like a surreal experience. I tried to be present and social, but my mind was thinking ahead and dreading the next day.

That night, my husband had a little too much to drink, so I drove us home not long after midnight. He was in rare form, slurring his words and insisting we were going the wrong way, even though he wasn't the one reading the map. Every few minutes, he'd wave his hands dramatically and exclaim, "Turn here!"—pointing in a completely wrong direction. Regan and I exchanged amused glances, unable to contain our laughter as he rambled on, convinced he knew a better route. At that moment, it was just silly, harmless fun. We laughed the whole way home, enjoying the ridiculousness of the situation. It felt good to have an easy, lighthearted night together.

Looking back, though, the memory isn't so simple. I've since become painfully aware of how my own choices—drinking, party-ing, normalizing alcohol as a way to unwind—may have shaped the way Regan viewed substances. At the time, it was all in good fun. But now, I wonder: did nights like these unintentionally send the wrong message? Did they make it easier for her to justify her own use later on? It's a complicated memory—one with both laughter and regret. But if nothing else, I am grateful for that brief moment of connection, however imperfect it may have been.

REGAN

I don't remember exactly what Mom said when she pulled in behind my car at Taylor's house. She definitely screamed at me, told me to go home, and said we would be having a talk. I went home and thought she had followed me, but I wasn't sure. What if she had already talked to Tim? He was going to be mad. And not only did I have drugs on me, but Taylor had left hers in my car, too. I hid what I could on myself, fully expecting Mom and Tim to go through all of my stuff—which Tim did immediately.

He was yelling, but I didn't even know what he was saying. I think I pretty much just got out of the car and walked straight inside without a word, like he wasn't even there. I don't even know if my car was still running because I don't think he let me shut the door or anything. He was already in the driveway, going through everything in my car. I know he found drugs, but it was all Taylor's, so I didn't care. I still had my own stash on me. I went to my room, quickly hid it all, and then I might have just passed out.

I don't think Tim ever came in to talk to me or really had any-thing to do with me after that. But I remember when Mom came in a while later. I had been doing LSD for two or three days in a row, so I was definitely still high. And as I was coming down from it, I felt so brain-dead. I don't really know how to explain it—just the worst head fog you could ever imagine, times a million. I knew what was going on, but I truly didn't care. So, I either passed out or had just lain down and was petting Sofi when Mom came in.

She was obviously angry, but I don't remember much of what she said. I just remember her asking if I was using and if I would pass a drug test. I told her no. Then she asked if I would stop. Again, I just said no.

At one point, she angrily threw my phone at me. Probably because I wasn't really giving her anything. I just didn't care. Then she said we were going to call my dad, and I had to tell him what was going on and that I wasn't coming back home.

In that instant, I remember hearing bells in my head, like, *This is amazing news! This is absolutely wonderful!* But then, I told myself to act like this was a bad thing, so I did. But in reality, I thought it was the best thing ever.

My dad and I didn't have this loving, close relationship. He didn't really care about me. Growing up, he had always been the fun parent, not the one enforcing rules. So now I was going to live with him, and it would basically be like having a roommate instead of a parent. I would go there, do whatever I wanted, and no one would be breathing down my neck.

This is so cool! I thought. *I can finally just do my drugs in peace and have everybody leave me alone.* It was the best idea I'd ever heard.

After that phone call, Mom basically told me to pack up everything I could fit on the plane because I wasn't coming back. That had me feeling pretty chipper, so I got up and started packing immediately. I was *so* ready for this. *This is great*, I thought. I was still packing when Mom and Tim left for their little trip.

Throughout my whole life, Dad was never one to be in my business. So, after they left, I called him. We kind of went over what had happened, and I'm pretty sure I told him, "Oh, she's mad because I've just been smoking a little bit of weed here and there, you know, and that's *drugs* to her or something." I completely lied, making it sound like that was all it was.

He said, "If that's all it is, and you're really not doing it all the time, I guess I don't really see a huge deal about that."

"Well, she sure does, so I don't know what her problem is," I told him, setting up the situation to benefit me once I got there. If he believed I was just smoking weed occasionally, I figured he wouldn't catch on to the truth—at least not for a while.

Next, I called Olivia, a friend from junior high that I always loved, even though, at that point, we weren't hanging out much or even speaking at all. I asked if she wanted to go to the lake park nearby to smoke. I told her I had some weed and stuff to talk about. She was happy to go; it was just the two of us. I filled her in on everything—how I was leaving in a couple of days, how my mom said I wasn't coming back. I told her I was actually really happy about it, but I wanted to see her one last time because I loved her. We sat, smoked, and had a good conversation. I hugged her goodbye, and that was that.

I didn't say anything to Sara or Taylor—just Olivia. Looking back, I don't even know why. Olivia was still in that old friend group I had stopped hanging out with months before, so I don't know what compelled me to only call her. I didn't know where we stood or whether she would even answer my call, but I just really wanted to say goodbye to her.

What's funny is that, even though I was home alone that night, I didn't feel compelled to go on some crazy bender. Without my parents at home, my mind could quiet down without drugs. It was *them* that pissed me off. It was *them* who made me so hurt and angry. And after seeing Olivia, I felt totally fine about leaving. No other goodbyes. No other cares in the world.

I had a good night and the next day by myself with Sofi at home. It was quiet—almost too quiet—but I didn't mind. I curled up with her, watched TV, and just existed without anyone around to bother me. No expectations, no lectures, no pretending. Just me and my dog.

I don't really remember Mom and Tim coming home, but obviously, they did. I must have said hello and gone about my business. I barely remember the New Year's party we went to, except for holding a baby. There's a picture of me doing that, so I know it happened.

One moment that stuck with me—one that I kept coming back to—was a fight that happened the year before at Christmas. I had gone to spend a week or so at Dad's in Illinois first. When I got there, I found a letter from Jacob on the guest bed where I'd be sleeping. I hadn't really talked to him in a while, and our relationship wasn't great at that point, so when I saw my name on that envelope, my heart practically stopped. I ripped it open, barely able to believe that he had left something for me. As I read his words, tears streamed down my face. I must've read the whole thing at least three times, clutching the paper like it was something fragile and precious.

In the letter, he told me how sorry he was for everything he had done to me, how much I didn't deserve any of it. He said he loved me so much that there was nothing I could ever do to make him hate me. He admitted he was disappointed in himself for the way he had treated me. It was everything I needed to hear. Everything I had been waiting for.

For the first time in what felt like forever, I had hope. I thought,

Oh my God, he loves me again. Maybe things would finally be okay. Maybe we could have the kind of relationship we used to have.

After about a week, Dad drove me to my grandma's house in Iowa to meet up with Mom, Tim, and the rest of the family. It didn't take long before they were all asking about Jacob. He hadn't spoken to any of them in over six months, and all I really told them was that he was going to boot camp soon. That should have been enough, but it wasn't. Everyone started pressing me for more—more details, more answers, more information that I *didn't want to give*.

Then, suddenly, it felt like they were all against me. They were yelling, demanding to know more, and I felt completely cornered. I started crying and ran downstairs to get away from them, my heart racing. Nobody understood that I was trying so hard to have a relationship with my brother again, but he didn't *want* me to tell them anything. He had trusted me to keep things between us, and I wasn't going to betray him.

For the past year, I had felt trapped in the middle of this war between my family and my brother, and I never knew what to do. Everyone wanted answers, and I had none that I could give. But Jacob was everything to me. He had always been my person, and I just wanted to make him happy. I thought that if I did everything *right* and if I proved my loyalty to him, he would finally love me again.

But instead, all I got was anger. No matter what I did, *somebody* was mad at me.

After that Christmas, my relationship with Jacob was nothing but back and forth, on again, off again. I never knew where I stood with him, and that entire year felt like my heart was being shattered over and over again.

I know people saw me as just this kid who skipped school and did drugs. But I was going through so much more than that. Looking back, I honestly believe that if my relationship with Jacob had stayed intact—if I hadn't lost him—I think I would have held myself together a lot better. Even with all the conflict and chaos in my family, I could have been okay. Because for so long, he was *all I needed*. I thought if I had him, nothing else mattered.

Losing him shattered me into a million pieces.

Chapter 6
Life at Dad's

The next morning, I drove Regan to the airport in Houston to catch her flight to Phoenix. We both knew this wasn't just another trip—it was the beginning of something uncertain, something neither of us could predict. But still, we pretended. We chatted about insignificant things, avoiding anything that would acknowledge the elephant in the car. I forced a cheerful tone, determined not to let my sadness spill over and make this any harder than it already was. If she was scared, she didn't show it. If I were falling apart, I wouldn't let her see it.

At seventeen, she was old enough to go through security on her own. I hugged her tight, breathing her in like I could somehow bottle up this moment and make it last. "I love you, baby girl," I whispered. She squeezed me back, "I love you, too," and then, just like that, she turned away. I stood frozen as she made her way through the line, my eyes locked on her until I physically couldn't see her anymore. Then, I finally let the tears fall. My chest ached as I walked to my car, my legs heavy, my mind screaming that this wasn't real. How had we gotten here? How was I driving away without her?

She texted me as always—first to say she had made it to her gate, then again when she was boarding. A small comfort in the middle of my unraveling. Her dad and I had agreed that she could keep her phone for the trip, but whether he would take it back once she arrived was up to him. It felt like such a small detail in the grand scheme of things. My drive home was silent, the weight of everything pressing down on me like a thick fog. The future stretched ahead of me, unfamiliar and empty.

By the time I pulled into the driveway, she was somewhere in the air, on her way to Arizona, on her way to a life I could no longer control or protect her from. Tim did his best to comfort me, his arms wrapping around me as I buried my face in his chest, but no words could make this better. Sofi clung to me, restless and uneasy, as if she felt the shift, too. The house was eerily quiet, suffocating in its stillness. The Christmas decorations that once filled our home with warmth now felt like a cruel joke. The joy of the season had been stripped away, leaving behind nothing but an ache I couldn't escape.

Between her dad and me, we handled the process of unenrolling her from her high school in Texas and getting her registered at her new school in Cottonwood, Arizona. Since I had given Regan her phone back to take with her, her dad confiscated it and told me he had gone over the rules and expectations for her staying with him. She started school a week after arriving, and they made plans to fly back that Saturday to get Sofi, her car, and the rest of her things. I set my sights on going through everything she'd packed to make sure there were no drugs in there. Truth be told, I really didn't want to know, and I prayed that I wouldn't find anything. I still couldn't believe any of this was happening. What I found was a vape, vape cartridges, two lighters, belly button piercing rings, and a Bic pen with tin foil on the end that had black residue on it. I took photos of it all and sent them to her dad. My gut knew this was not good, but my brain just didn't want to believe there was really a drug problem. She was just experimenting and needed to find new friends and start a new life away from whatever and whoever was influencing her.

The awkwardness in the car was suffocating, filling every inch of space between us. Regan sat quietly in the back seat while Greg took the front next to me. It had been years since we'd all been together like this, and the forced small talk only made it more apparent just how fractured everything had become.

"So, how was the flight?" I asked, my voice overly chipper in an attempt to smooth the rough edges of the moment.

"Good," Greg replied flatly, barely looking at me. "Long."

I nodded, unsure of what else to say. Regan chimed in about how excited she was to see Sofi, and I latched onto that, asking about her, about Arizona, about anything that felt remotely safe. She answered, but there was a detachment in her tone, as if she were hovering just outside of the conversation, giving me what I wanted to hear but not offering anything more. Greg kept checking his watch, impatient to get back on the road, back to the life where she now existed without me.

The silence stretched, and I reached for something familiar, something grounding. For most of the forty-five-minute drive, I turned up the praise and worship music, letting the lyrics fill the car, hoping—praying—that maybe it would perform miracles in them both.

When we got to the house, there was no pause, no moment to breathe. Regan and Greg immediately set to work, carrying out her things and packing up her car. I stood there, watching as my daughter's presence in my home was reduced to bags and boxes, methodically loaded up as if she were just another errand to check off a list. The whole experience felt surreal, as if I were watching it unfold from outside my own body.

And then, just like that, it was time. She stood in front of me, my baby girl, looking at me with those same eyes that had always melted my heart. I hugged her tightly, trying to hold onto her, even if just for a second longer. "I love you, Regan," I whispered. "I hope you're making better choices."

"I love you too, Mom," she said, her voice soft but steady. She was sweet, affectionate—still mine. But she was leaving. I stood in the driveway, my heart breaking as they pulled away, my hands gripping my arms as if holding myself together. The car disappeared down the street, and the house behind me suddenly felt unbearably empty. This was really happening.

The quiet in the house was deafening, pressing in on me the instant I walked back inside. It wasn't just silence—it was absence, thick and heavy, wrapping around me like a dense fog. At least with Sofi here, I had a small anchor, something to fill the space, a living presence to soften the emptiness. But without her, the house felt hollow, like a stage after the final curtain had dropped—lifeless, still, abandoned. I had become an empty nester overnight, and the suddenness of it hit me like bricks being placed on my chest, making it hard to breathe. I didn't know what to do with myself.

As the hours passed, I tracked Regan and her dad's drive back to Arizona since I could see her car's location. Oddly, they took the long way around, which made me uneasy. I texted Regan only to check in, and she simply replied that she was tired, bored, and ready to be out of the car. No surprise there.

This was significant. Empty nesting without warning was devastating. The silence in the house was deafening, and the absence of the everyday chaos I once took for granted felt like a weight pressing down on me. Within about forty-eight hours, I turned to my husband and said, "I want a dog." The pain of the stillness was unbearable, and I know he felt it, too, because he didn't even try to argue. He simply looked at me for a moment as if making sure I was certain and then asked, "Are you sure?"

"Yes," I said without hesitation.

"Okay," he replied without another word.

By the weekend, I had already scoured listings and found the puppy I wanted. Together, we went to get him—a tiny, eight-week-old Maltipoo and Shih Tzu mix. The moment I held him, I felt something in me soften just a little. I named him Charlie, and he became my comfort in the emptiness. His playful energy and unconditional love gave me something to pour myself into when I felt like I had nothing left to give. He brought me joy despite my broken heart.

I had no choice but to keep getting up and going to work and the gym and all the things I had done prior to Christmas, except for keeping track of Regan. She was gone, and while I desperately missed her, I felt at peace on some level that this was a chance for her to change her life and do things differently. I didn't think it was possible for her to do that here, and I couldn't think of anything else I could do for her. Every time I texted her or called, she was cheerful and told me everything in Arizona was great. This further made me feel that I'd made the right choice. She was making friends, particularly in her art class, going to church with her dad regularly, and had her cousins right next door that she could spend time with. It appeared that she was settling in nicely.

Even her dad told me on our weekly calls that she was doing

well there. I would call him each week to check in with him about how she was doing and what I could do to help. He always told me things were good, what they were doing, school was going well, etc. Knowing this made life easier for me to move forward. I thought we'd dodged a bullet and that she was going to be fine.

As Valentine's Day approached, I carefully put together a gift basket for Regan, filling it with things I thought would make her smile—framed photos, candy, hair ties, a soft heart-shaped pillow, and little trinkets to remind her of home. I was proud of it, excited to send it off, and even more excited for her to receive it. Lord, I missed her. The day after I had packed everything up and gotten it ready to ship, my phone buzzed with a text from her.

`Please don't be mad at me`

My stomach dropped. What? Before I could even type out a response, another message popped up. She explained she needed a change and that she *loved* it—she just hoped I would love it too. Then came the pictures.

I sucked in a breath. Her long, thick brown hair—*gone*. Cut within an inch or two from her head. Her hair had been everything to her for as long as I could remember. When she was little, I used to beg her to let me brush it or braid it, but she was so tender-headed she insisted on doing it herself. Even as she grew into a young woman, her hair was part of her identity, often reaching her waist before she would even trim it, something she took such pride in. And now, in a single afternoon, it was gone.

I know I didn't hide my bewilderment well. My fingers hovered over my phone, unsure of what to say.

`Well, as long as you love it, I love it too. It's your hair—you can do whatever you want with it`

I meant it, but it would take me some time to get used to it. Still unsettled, I immediately called her dad. He sounded just as surprised. "I had no idea she was going to do that," he admitted. "She just went to get a haircut and came back with no hair." He didn't seem concerned, at least not outwardly. But I was. I was freaked out, if I'm being honest. What in the world was going on? Yet, I had no choice but to dismiss it. I wasn't there. And they both kept saying she was doing well. I had to take them at their word.

A few days later, she called after receiving the Valentine's Day package. Her voice was full of excitement as she thanked me, then laughed, "Mom, you sent me a whole pack of hair ties... and I don't have any hair!" I chuckled along with her, but something about her next statement struck me. *Nobody had ever sent her anything like that before. It made her feel special.* That comment sat heavy in my heart, but I pushed it aside. She sounded happy, and that's what mattered. I told myself to focus on that.

I kept in regular contact with both Regan and her dad, though my longer conversations were mostly with him. Over time, I could sense his growing annoyance—he never said anything outright, but after knowing him since I was nineteen, I could read his tone as clearly as if it were written on a page. Still, he remained polite, answering my questions, though with less enthusiasm each time. I ignored the shift, unwilling to let it deter me. Staying involved in my daughter's life—however much I could from a distance—was not something I was willing to compromise.

Spring break was approaching in mid-March, so I asked if it would be okay for Regan to come for a short visit. He told me he didn't have anything against it, but that he would have to ask her if she wanted to. I'd already mentioned it to her, and she was agreeable to coming for a few days. I wouldn't say she was excited about it, but she was polite and said she would come. I booked her flights for Sunday through Wednesday, knowing four days was likely all I could handle. She couldn't see any of her old friends, and I had to work, which meant she'd be stuck coming with me unless I could find something "safe" for her to do. The excitement of seeing her grew, but so did my anxiety. I wasn't sure I could trust her, and I couldn't risk giving her an opportunity to make me regret having her visit. The worry gnawed at me, a silent battle between wanting to believe in her and fearing the worst. Still, I was determined to navigate it. The thought of not seeing her felt even harder to bear. All would be well.

The morning before she was to fly to Houston, she told her dad she didn't want to come. He called me to tell me this, which upset me. Why didn't she want to come? I had already bought the plane tickets weeks ago! His response was vague in that he just said she was refusing to go, and he was not going to argue with her, so it was up to me to figure it out. I told him it was his responsibility to get her to the airport, as it had been mine for the past ten years. He told me angrily that he wasn't going to be the "bad guy" in this for making her do something she didn't want to do. That statement caught me off guard, and for some reason, it still lingers with me. There was an edge to his voice—something sharp, defensive, and distant—that I couldn't quite make sense of at the time.

When I called her, she was very sorry but also adamant that she no longer wanted to come. She said she wanted to stay there and spend time with her friends instead. I didn't intend to argue with her, so I worked on persuading her that we would have a good time and that I'd already paid for her flights. She wasn't budging, and time was of the essence. As we talked, I began to assure her that I would keep her safe and that I wouldn't let anything or anyone hurt her while she was with us. She began to cry, which surprised me, but I pressed on, asking her what she was afraid of. She never gave me much of an answer, but she did eventually agree to come, and she kept her word. It was a very strange conversation and situation, one we never addressed or revisited again.

When I picked her up from the airport on Sunday evening, I was happy to see her, but noticed she was still dressing in drab, baggy clothing, and her hair was just horrifically short. She acted happy to see me, though, and that was nice, but she also made plans on our drive home to see her ex-boyfriend. He was coming to our house shortly after we would get there. This was not a great idea in my book, but I also knew that he was not a drug user, so at least that wasn't something to worry about. However, the whole arrangement was unsettling, as he showed up around 9 p.m., and they sat outside talking on our steps for the next several hours. I checked on them off and on, worried something else was going on, but he did eventually leave, and she went to sleep in her room on top of the covers.

Our visit was really nice—simple but meaningful. I took her to the doctor for a well visit, attempted (unsuccessfully) to get a new retainer to replace the one she lost, and helped her complete her FAFSA for college. The everyday tasks made it feel, for a moment, like things were normal again. But my favorite part of her visit was Wednesday, when she spent the entire day at my office with me. I knew it wasn't her idea of a great time, but she didn't complain. We chatted and listened to music, and there was an ease to our conversations.

She was still my sweet girl—polite, agreeable, with flashes of the warmth I had missed so much. At one point, I told her how grateful I was that she had come and how much it meant to me. She smiled, giving me one of her tight, lingering hugs. "I'm glad I got on that plane," she reassured me. I was, too.

Before we left for the airport, I slipped her $172 tax refund check into an envelope with her dad's name on it, telling her to give it to him when she got home. Neither he nor I trusted her with money yet, though we never actually voiced why. Some things didn't need to be said.

Saying goodbye was hard, as always, but this time felt different. She seemed okay, and for the first time in a long time, I was, too. I was settling into my own new routine, carving out a life that wasn't centered around worry and fear. Still, when I got back home from the airport, the quiet was deafening.

She returned to Arizona on Wednesday night without any issues. What happened over the next week still blows my mind. I may never know what truly happened in her head after that visit back to Texas, but something must've shifted dramatically. Or, I had been deceived from the get-go. Maybe a bit of both.

The following day, I received a message from Greg asking if I had a few minutes to talk. He had received Regan's report card for the first quarter of school, and she was failing English and math and had only completed 13% of her economics online course. There had been no math or English assignments turned in for weeks, and her dad had not been checking up on her. This was news to me! She never mentioned having trouble in school. In fact, she had said she was doing fine in school. My suspicion was that she was sabotaging herself, afraid to succeed, and choosing to fail. He didn't want me to talk to her about it yet, so I didn't. I made suggestions to him about meeting with her teachers, asking for extra credit, monitoring her work, etc. All the things a parent does to make sure their child succeeds and graduates on time. He said he would do that as soon as spring break was over on Monday.

Monday evening, Greg messaged me again, asking if I had a

minute to talk. This was becoming a pattern. I could almost picture him—pacing in his living room, rubbing his forehead in frustration, his voice laced with that same mix of irritation and anger I had come to recognize over the years. On the phone, he got straight to the point: "Regan didn't come home from school." His tone was clipped and controlled, but I could hear the underlying edge of concern. He explained they had argued over her grades, and as a result, he had grounded her—no going out, only school and home. But now, she wasn't answering his texts or calls. "She told me she'd come home when she's ready," he admitted. Instantly, I knew this was bad. My pulse quickened, and I gripped the phone tighter. "Do you know which friends she might be with?" He didn't.

"What about places in town she likes to hang out?" He didn't know. My stomach sank.

"Have you checked the tracking program?" I asked, already knowing the answer.

"I, uh… I haven't looked at how to do that yet."

I held my breath, willing myself to stay calm and not start an argument by saying what was really on my mind. I had set everything up for him the moment she moved in. He had all the information but hadn't bothered to use it. "Okay," I said, exhaling sharply. "Let me check." Within minutes, I pulled up the address and read it off to him, my heart pounding.

I waited over an hour and a half to hear if he found her, and finally asked him. He said her car was right where I said it was, sitting at a house that looked like there was nobody home except for her car being there. He went to the front door, rang the doorbell, and knocked, but nobody answered. After waiting fifteen minutes, he left and went back home. He didn't know whose house it was, but assumed it must belong to a girl whom she'd been spending time with recently. A couple of hours went by before I received another message from him that read:

```
I had to call the cops tonight
```

What transpired in those few hours was something I could never have imagined. He described our daughter finally arriving home that night and going to her room while he was letting her know how displeased he was with her defiant behavior. He noticed she'd parked her car down the street, which was unusual. She shut and locked her bedroom door while she packed up her clothes. During the argument, he threatened to break down her door when she refused to let him in, and he did so, which escalated things further. She continued to finish packing and told him she was leaving. There were friends waiting in her car to help her escape. I'm not sure at what point the police were called to the house, but I was filled in after the fact.

The police officers talked to both of them and explained that since she was still seventeen years old, if she ran away, they would find her and have to bring her back home. She told them all she would not stay there and intended to leave the first chance she got.

She was angry and defiant, even to the officers. Greg called me while the officer was talking to Regan privately. Her friends were ordered to leave the property, which they promptly did. He relayed to me what had happened to that point and that he was fearful that she would leave in the middle of the night while he was asleep. He was not sure what to do. She had clearly been using drugs, but who knows what drugs, how much, or even for how long?

The three of us had a conversation after the officers left. Regan remained angry and defiant, blaming us for her problems and for not letting her go. She was particularly angry at her dad and even insulted her uncle and cousins, whom she had always expressed love for previously. It was like she was a different person—someone I didn't recognize. I'm not sure we really resolved anything that night, but clearly, some action needed to be taken. She was not only grounded but also needed to be on lockdown, and I wasn't there to be of much help.

That night, out of sheer desperation, I started looking at drug treatment centers. I had no idea what I was searching for—I didn't even know if she truly needed rehab—but we needed help. She was spiraling, and I felt powerless to stop it. My knowledge of drugs and treatment was nonexistent, but what I did know was that my daughter was in crisis, and whatever road she was on, she was speeding down it at a hundred miles per hour. I prayed—pleading with God to show me what to do, to help me help her—while my tired eyes scoured Google search results for hours.

The more I searched, the more disheartened I became. Resources for teens using drugs were frustratingly limited, and most programs I found were in other states. I wasn't about to send her somewhere far away and alone. I kept narrowing my search to Arizona and Texas, but the options were slim. Still, one name kept appearing in the results, no matter what I typed: "The Pathway Program" in Tempe, Arizona. Something about it caught my attention. Was this a sign? A nudge from above?

I sent the information to Greg that night, along with a few articles I had found on how marijuana affects the brain—how its increased potency had led to a sixty-eight percent rise in emergency room visits, how it could cause aggression and personality changes. I wasn't even sure what I believed about it all, but I needed him to see what I was seeing. We agreed that we needed to find a drug counselor for her, though we both feared she would refuse to participate. If things didn't change, we might have to take more drastic steps.

Ultimately, Greg decided to search Regan's room after she left for school the next morning. I spent that Tuesday consumed with worry, the weight of the previous night pressing down on me as we debated the next steps. Taking her car keys, her computer, and her phone seemed like logical consequences, but each came with complications. She needed her laptop for school—how could we restrict its use without completely cutting her off from what she needed? Every decision felt impossible, every solution riddled with questions I didn't know how to answer.

Desperate for guidance, I turned to Google, again scouring search results for treatment options while Greg spoke with a pastor at his church. I picked up the phone and started calling places to ask the same desperate questions: *How do we even know if our daughter needs treatment? What does that even look like? Will she be able to finish school? What about college? Will this help her like herself again?*

But mostly, *please, just tell me what to do. Tell me how to save my daughter.*

One after another, my calls went to voicemail, automated messages directing me to leave my number for a callback that never came. My heart sank deeper with every hour that passed in silence. *Does nobody care? Is there no help for us?*

Then, finally, someone answered. A man named Kyle at The Pathway Program. His voice was calm, steady, and confident— soothing my frayed nerves as he explained that they specialized in working with teens just like Regan. He directed me to their website, which I had already combed through in my frantic searching, and assured me that when we were ready, they could help. I thanked him, still holding out hope that one of my other messages would be returned. But as the hours stretched on and the silence remained, I started to wonder—*Was this the answer to my prayers?*

Greg's pastor recommended a place called the "Dream Center" in Los Angeles, CA, and strongly recommended we find treatment for our daughter. My gut told me that sending my seventeen-year-old to LA was not something I could do, and luckily, Greg respected my reluctance. We still hoped that she would turn things around, and that none of this would end up being necessary. I suggested playing Christian music in the house twenty-four-seven, which he said he already was doing. Thinking back now, that sounds ridiculous, but we were truly grasping at straws.

That evening, the climate in Greg's home can only be described as hostile. Regan was mad at the world and at him and had no problem taking it out on him. She resorted to giving him the silent treatment all evening.

The silent treatment continued Wednesday morning. Regan actually got up early, got ready for school, and left the house without a word, walking to school on her own. Greg was obviously worried she'd run away, but found her at school that morning. He argued with her about leaving without telling him, but she was steadfast in her defiance and maintained that she was at school and had work to do, effectively dismissing him. He picked her up from school that day and agreed to let her stay at her uncle's house instead of their house with him. She wanted nothing to do with him, so I suppose this was a way to give them both time apart. They had Bible Study that night at church, and he'd told me she liked going to that, so I was hopeful that might spark a change in her behavior. But they never made it to Bible Study.

Instead, I received a phone call early that evening from Greg, who was crying. I went out to my driveway, needing some air, to find out what in the world was wrong. Historically, our relationship was lacking in the communication department, but when we did talk, he was often short, snarky, and showed little emotion. For my ex-husband to be on the other end of the phone in tears was hard for me to process—I was the last person on earth this man wanted to be this vulnerable with.

"What's going on?" I asked, pushing aside my astonishment, trying to keep my voice steady. His words tumbled out in pieces as he began to explain. He told me he'd gone to pick up Regan from his brother's house at the agreed-upon time, but she refused to leave. When he insisted, she defied him outright. His frustration escalated, and in an effort to force her out, he grabbed her. She fought back. He ended up pinning her to the floor, and in that moment, everything came pouring out of her. She told him she hated him. That he was never a father to her. That he had always loved her brother more. That he was the reason she was the way she was. I closed my eyes, feeling the weight of those words like a sharp wind cutting straight through me. I knew her words had stung hard.

On the other end of the line, Greg was breaking apart. "I think she meant it," he admitted, his voice raw, void of the arrogance and indifference I'd come to expect from him. For years, I had been the one carrying the weight of his actions—his manipulation, his cruelty, his relentless efforts to turn my own daughter against me. And yet, at this moment, when it all came back to him when he was finally forced to sit in the consequences of his choices, I couldn't even bring myself to feel triumphant. I should have felt justified. I should have felt some kind of satisfaction that he was finally seeing the damage he had done. But all I felt was compassion and sadness.

"She doesn't hate you," I said quietly, forcing my voice to be softer than I expected it to be. "She's angry. She's hurting. But she doesn't hate you."

He exhaled shakily, but I could tell he wasn't convinced. "I don't know," he muttered. "I think she does." I didn't argue. Maybe she did mean it. Maybe she didn't. Either way, the damage was done.

And then he said the words that made my breath catch in my throat. "I can't do this anymore. She's out of control. What if she tells someone—tells the police—that I did something I didn't do? I don't know what she's capable of."

I gripped the phone tighter, feeling the weight of his panic settle into my own chest. The ground beneath me felt unsteady. "I don't think I can risk having her here," he said finally, his voice quieter now, more certain. I swallowed hard. I wasn't ready for her to come back home to Texas. But it wasn't about what I was ready for anymore. We had reached a point we had started to plan for, but never thought would come. At least, I didn't think it would.

Just as my conversation with her dad was wrapping up, my phone lit up with Regan's name. My stomach tightened. I knew before I even answered that she would be in tears. "Mom," she sobbed. "He attacked me. I hate him. I want nothing to do with him. Can I come home?" Her words hit me like a wrecking ball—full of pain, desperation, and anger. I ached to say yes, to tell her to come home where I could protect her, but I couldn't. As much as I loved her, I couldn't let drugs back into our home. I forced myself to say it. "As long as you're using drugs, you can't come back home." For a few seconds in the silence that followed, I thought she might fight me on it, but she didn't. Instead, she muttered, "I won't be staying here much longer." I let the words hang in the air, their implication clear—she was planning to run. My heart pounded, but I knew pressing her would only push her further away. Right now, my job wasn't to solve everything. It was to love her, listen, and keep her from making another rash decision.

Gently, I coaxed her back to her dad's house with the promise that she could have some space—just her and Sofi, alone in her room for the night. I asked Greg to leave her be and give her time to breathe. He agreed, though we both knew this wasn't a real solution. It was a temporary Band-Aid over a wound that was only getting deeper.

As soon as I hung up, the only thing I could think of to do was to call Pathway. "Can she meet with Kyle tomorrow?"

"Four o'clock," they told me. I exhaled, a small wave of relief washing over me. It wasn't a perfect plan, but it was a step forward.

REGAN

I knew that after I packed up my entire bedroom, Mom would go through everything before I could come back to pick it up. I don't remember exactly where I had hidden it, but I had two or three different pipes for smoking, a grinder full of weed, a baggie of weed, and my vape—all stashed in the car while Dad and I drove back to Arizona. The stuff Mom did find was old, stuff I didn't care about. But everything I actually wanted to keep was hidden somewhere in my room, not in the boxes and bags I had packed. She must've only checked those.

At some point, I was able to slip everything into my purse when nobody was looking. Dad had no clue I had drugs with us the entire nineteen-hour drive. The whole time, I couldn't wait to get to Arizona so I could finally smoke. It was a long trip without using.

When I first got to my dad's, they immediately started throwing me into the church scene, introducing me to all their friends. I really didn't want to do any of it. They were all so peppy and annoying. One girl, in particular, kept talking to me. Nobody seemed to like her, but no one would say anything to her either—it was a small town. She kept asking questions, trying to make conversation.

She was like, "I run track! Do you run track?"

"No," I said, already annoyed.

"Well, do you play sports?"

"No."

She wouldn't let it go. "Have you ever played sports?"

"Yeah."

"What sport?"

"Beach volleyball."

"Oh! Well, you should run track!"

I just looked at her and, probably way too rudely, told her, "I'm not going to do that."

She didn't really talk to me after that.

I also met Rue. He was in my grade, and he was probably the only person there who didn't seem fake. He was genuinely nice, super chill, and kind of shy.

At school, I knew there had to be a messed-up crowd somewhere—the people who partied and smoked. And I was going to find them. So I spent the first week pretending to be happy, making sure I met as many people as possible. It didn't take long.

I met a girl who was obviously a stoner, and she invited me over to hang out. I don't even remember her name. There was no hesitation—I told Dad about it (leaving out the smoking part), and he was just happy I was making friends. When I got there, she had two guy friends over, also in our grade. They were smoking and doing whatever, and when they offered me some, I pulled out my own stash and smoked. Honestly, I don't remember much after that.

My cousin, who was a few years younger than I, had just started playing volleyball, and for a while, I was the one driving her to practice and hanging out with her a lot. I helped teach her how to play, and I did enjoy that—she looked up to me like an older sister, and that felt good. But as much as I liked being with her, I wanted to get back to my people and what I was really trying to do there. I wanted to be with my friends, getting high.

Dad, on the other hand, wanted to cook dinner every night or take me out to eat, and he kept trying to plan things for us to do. At first, I didn't mind too much—it was a new place, and I was getting familiar with my surroundings. But pretty quickly, it started to annoy me. I wasn't here to hang out with him. I was here to do whatever I wanted.

In my mind, the plan was simple: I'd live there, stay out of his business, and he'd stay out of mine. We'd never really been involved in each other's lives before, so why should that change now? But apparently, that wasn't how he saw things. And it started pissing me off because he was getting in the way of me doing drugs.

I had never felt like he really cared about me enough to want to spend time with me before. We never did things like that when I was younger, so why now? What was different? Part of me wondered if he was catching on or if he was starting to suspect something. I don't know exactly when he realized I was using, but I wasn't home much anymore. I was always out doing whatever I wanted while he was trying to set rules for the house—rules that I had no intention of following.

He kept telling me I couldn't stay out all night and couldn't just come and go whenever I pleased. And I kept telling him, "Yes, I can."

The biggest rule he tried to put in place was a 10 p.m. curfew.

That wasn't happening. One night, after coming home late again—after multiple nights of completely ignoring his rule—I walked in to find him sitting on the couch, waiting up for me.

"I told you to be home by ten," he said.

I just shrugged. "Oh well. I told you I wasn't going to be home by ten." Then I walked straight to my room and shut the door.

At that point, I don't think either of us liked each other very much. And after that, he stopped trying to take me to lunch or do things with me.

I was mostly smoking weed and drinking some while I was out there. I also did mushrooms. One night, after I had done mushrooms and smoked quite a bit, I was nowhere near sober when I called Rue. I called Rue often, and maybe he reminded me of Jacob in some way, but he was just a genuinely good person. I never really understood why he cared about me or wanted to be my friend because, from the first day I arrived, it was obvious I didn't have my s*** together.

That night, my dad and I had been fighting pretty badly, and I just couldn't handle it. So I called Rue and asked if he could meet me, and he did. I felt a little guilty because he wasn't the type of person who would ever think about trying drugs, and I hated the idea of bringing that into his life—of him having to see me like that. But I got in his truck at Sonic, and we just sat there. I was apologizing to him, telling him I didn't know what was wrong with me. I don't remember what he said, but I do remember that anytime I needed him, he showed up.

Pretty soon, I settled into a routine: wake up in the morning, go to my friend's house to smoke while she finished getting ready for school, and then we'd go together. We had art class at eleven, and sometimes, that was the only class we'd show up for. Most of the time, we'd just leave. I was using most of the day, every day, and barely attending school. I don't think my dad ever knew that. For a couple of weeks, my uncle hired me to do some filing at his office after school, and I actually did that.

At the end of January, after only being in Arizona for four weeks, I needed a change. Call it a midlife crisis, I don't know. I went and bought box bleach and bleached my hair. I didn't like it, so I did it again the next day. I still didn't like it, so I bought a box of dark brown hair dye and went really dark. But even that wasn't enough. A week later, I walked into a local salon and told the stylist, "I want it all gone."

I didn't do it because I really wanted short hair. I did it to give the middle finger to everyone in my life. I would have gone even shorter, but the stylist refused. She said my hair was too long, and she was afraid I'd regret it. She asked if I at least wanted to donate it, and I told her, "I don't want any of it. I don't care what you do with it. Just get it off my head."

I have no memory of visiting my mom over spring break. I know I did because I've seen pictures of it, but clearly, my drug use was messing with my memory. There are so many things I don't remember or that feel vague and blurry. But I do have pictures of me using after I got back to my dad's.

After that trip, things felt even more out of control. I was obviously getting high, but one particular day, I started telling my friends everything I was dealing with, how much I hated being there, and that I didn't want to do it anymore. Right then, I decided I was leaving. And as stupid as we all were, they jumped on board, telling me it was a great idea. We made a plan to go to my dad's and pack my stuff, and then I'd stay with my friend for the night until we figured out the rest.

We drove to my house, and when I got to my room, I immediately opened my dresser and started shoving clothes into a bag. Dad was talking—maybe yelling—but I tuned him out completely. I wasn't listening, and I wasn't answering. I just waited for him to leave me alone. When he didn't, I slammed the door shut and locked it. He banged on it, demanding that I open up. I refused. That just made him even angrier.

The next thing I knew, there was a loud crack as my door flew open—he had kicked it in.

I jumped back, heart racing, and screamed at him to get out. "You're a psycho! Just shut up! Shut up, shut up, shut up!"

He kept yelling, but I didn't even know what he was saying. All I knew was that I had to get out of there.

Then, suddenly, two cops were in my room.

I was sitting on my bed, crying, still trying to catch my breath. One of them crouched down and started asking me questions. "Is he hurting you?" "Did he put his hands on you?"

I didn't answer at first. I just kept shaking my head, muttering, "He's crazy. I need to get away from him."

They told me, "Well, you can't run away, you know. If you do, we're just going to have to bring you back because you're seventeen."

I looked them straight in the eye and said, "Guess I'll see you again tonight, then."

I don't really remember what happened after that. I must've agreed to calm down or something because the cops eventually left. I don't remember talking to my dad again, either. I just knew I wasn't staying.

I lay in bed with my phone, texting my friends. "Just waiting for him to fall asleep," I told them. "Then I'll climb out the window and meet you down the street." I was so close to being free.

But then, as I was lying there, thinking through my plan, my eyes got heavy. I tried to fight it, but I must've passed out.

When I woke up the next morning, the house was already quiet, which meant Dad was up. Crap. I fell asleep. That really sucks.

He took my car keys the night before, and now he was making some big speech about how he'd be driving me everywhere from now on. "You're grounded. You'll go to school, and you'll come straight home. No car. No phone." Blah, blah, blah.

In my head, I was thinking, *Sure you are.*

But for the moment, I let him believe he had won. He drove me to school that day, and for once, I actually stayed the whole time. Part of me figured that in a town this small, the cops were probably watching me now. Without my car or my phone, I had no choice but to accept defeat. At least for now.

The following day, I got creative. Since I didn't have anything—no drugs, no phone, no car—I grabbed Sofi's leash and took her for a walk. I never really walked her before, but that day, it became my excuse. I walked her all the way to my friend's house, got high, and then walked back home at some point. Dad never said much about my long walks, so I kept doing it.

The day after that, I decided that if I had to accept defeat, I was going to do it on my own terms. I set my alarm clock extra early, got up quietly, and made sure I was ready for school before Dad even woke up. Then, I walked. By the time the first-period bell rang, I was sitting at my desk, minding my own business, actually doing my work.

And then I heard it.

Dad's voice, loud and demanding, echoed down the hallway: **"Where is she?"**

A few student aides were with him, and suddenly, all eyes were on me. I was in the corner of the classroom, staring at my computer screen, pretending not to notice him making a spectacle of himself. I could feel the confusion from everyone in the room—what was this guy so mad about? His daughter was literally in school, doing what she was supposed to do.

For the first time in a long time, I felt a little victorious. I wanted to smile. Hell, I wanted to laugh. Not only did I completely ignore his rules, but now he looked ridiculous for being angry at me for *being in school.*

I kept my expression neutral as he stormed up to me, his voice quieter now. "I told you that I would be taking you and picking you up from school."

I still didn't look up from my computer. "Please don't interrupt me. I'm trying to do my schoolwork."

I could feel the rage simmering under his skin, but he didn't say another word. He just turned and left.

The next day, still pretending to accept defeat, I let him take me to school and pick me up, but I made it painfully clear that I wanted nothing to do with him. After school, I went to my uncle's house instead of going home. I didn't want to be near my dad; at least there, I could be left alone. I went into my cousin's room, sat on the floor, and pulled out my laptop, thinking that I might as well get caught up on schoolwork since I had nothing better to do.

At some point, Dad showed up. I ignored him at first, but he was already angry. "You need to leave. Now."

I didn't even look up. "I'm doing my schoolwork."

"Get up."

"Leave me alone," I shot back.

I could tell my defiance pushed him over the edge. His voice got sharper. "If you don't get up, I'll drag you out of here myself."

I stayed where I was, refusing to move.

The next second, he lunged at me.

Panic surged through me, and I started kicking, punching, slapping—whatever I could do to get him *off* of me. But he was stronger, and before I knew it, he had me pinned down on the floor. I thrashed underneath him, screaming, cussing, telling him to *get the f*** off me.

Then, in a split second, it was like time stopped. I looked down the hallway and saw my cousin standing there, watching. For a moment, we locked eyes. Then, without a word, he turned and walked into the bathroom, turning on the shower.

That's when Dad said, "What is wrong with you?"

All of the anger came out of me at that moment, and I couldn't hold it back. I let it all out. The words exploded from me, years of pain and anger bubbling to the surface in one unstoppable stream.

"I hate you. You were never a dad to me. You always favored Jacob, and you're the reason why he's depressed and suicidal. You're the reason why I want to kill myself. You're the reason I'm a f***ing drug addict!"

He didn't say a word. Not one.

He just got up and left.

I don't remember anything after that.

At some point that night or the next morning, I must've gotten my phone back because Mom called me during my art class. I stepped out to answer, and that's when she told me about Pathway. I didn't care where she wanted to send me. I just wanted to be away from my dad. It wasn't about getting sober. It wasn't about going to rehab. If she had said I was going to boot camp or boarding school, I would've agreed to that, too. I just needed *out*.

So, I told her I'd gladly go to the meeting after school.

Once I knew I was leaving for good, I made sure to go find my friends. I got high, told them I was being "shipped away," and said my goodbyes.

"I'm out of here," I told them. And I meant it.

Chapter 7
The Pathway Program

Thursday morning arrived after another sleepless night. My stomach was in knots from the moment I got up, knowing this day could change everything—or nothing at all. It was going to be an agonizingly long one for me, waiting for Regan and Greg's meeting with Kyle. Since 4:00 p.m., my time was only 2:00 p.m. in Arizona, I wouldn't know anything until after 6:00 p.m. The hours stretched endlessly at work. I tried to stay busy, but my mind kept drifting back to my phone, willing it to ring with an update.

Greg and I texted off and on throughout the day. That morning, he dropped Regan off at school as usual, though their interactions were as cold as ever. She barely acknowledged him, still refusing to speak to him unless absolutely necessary. The plan was for him to pick her up at 1:30 p.m. so they could make the two-and-a-half-hour drive to Tempe in time for their 4:00 p.m. appointment. He'd accounted for traffic, but there was no way to prepare for the tension in that car.

The drive was silent. Regan sat pressed against the passenger door, as physically far from her father as she could get. He didn't push, didn't try to force conversation. She had already made it clear—she wanted nothing to do with him. In fact, she had gone so far as to say she wanted to join Pathway's residential program just to get away from him. But we were holding onto hope that there would be an option for her to stay in the program while continuing to attend school and live at his house.

By 7:30 p.m., my patience was running thin. It had been an hour and a half, and I still hadn't heard a word. Finally, my phone rang. It was Greg. I could tell he was crying before he even spoke. "I'm on my way home," he said, "Alone."

My heart clenched. "What do you mean? What happened?"

He took a shaky breath before explaining. The meeting with Kyle had gone well—better than expected, actually. He liked Kyle, and surprisingly, Regan did, too. But while Greg was speaking with Kyle in private, Regan had been sitting in the waiting area when a group of teens—kids her age, all in the program—approached her. They were friendly, excited to meet her, and eager to pull her in.

"Are you coming here?" they'd asked.

She wasn't sure.

"You should stay the night with us! We're having a sleepover."

Regan didn't think it was a bad idea. "You'll have to ask my dad," she told them. "I'm not asking him."

The second Greg walked out of his meeting, the girls surrounded him, pleading on her behalf.

"Can she stay?"

"She really needs this."

"We'll take good care of her, promise!"

Greg had been caught off guard. He knew she didn't want to

come home with him. That had been painfully obvious. Standing there in that moment, he was torn between their pleading for her to stay and not knowing any of them well enough to feel good about saying yes.

He reluctantly agreed. But there was a problem. He couldn't come back the next day to pick her up, and she didn't have a phone.

"That's okay!" one of the girls had said. "She can stay the whole weekend."

"She can use one of our phones if she needs anything!"

Now, on the phone with me, Greg sounded lost. "I don't know if I did the right thing," he admitted.

I stared at the wall, trying to process. I didn't know either. But I did know that they both needed a break.

"She's safe," I said carefully. "And maybe some space is good for both of you." I wasn't sure if I was trying to convince him or myself.

He exhaled. "I'll go back to get her Sunday after church."

"Okay."

That was all we could do—wait. And while I waited, I kept searching, desperate for a way to make this work with school.

I didn't find any good options, but I did find confirmation that it was a good idea to have an adolescent go to treatment in a place that is unfamiliar to them. This minimizes the threat of running away and gives them time to focus on learning new skills, therapy, etc. Our biggest problem with the whole thing was having to drop out of high school, especially when she only had nine weeks to finish and graduate. We had a few days to digest this, but I felt a bit more hopeful when Regan left me a voicemail and called me twice after being there only twenty-four hours. She told me she loved it there, and being there was making her want to be clean.

She talked and talked about how great everyone and everything was, sounding happier than I'd heard her in what felt like a very long time. She even apologized to me for her behavior.

Greg sent me a breakdown of the cost of the program. We did not have insurance that would cover any of it, so we had to determine if we could afford it and how. It was a two-and-a-half-year program for a one-time cost of several thousand dollars; the total depended on whether she would be in Step Two (residential treatment for those under eighteen) or start with IOP (Intensive Outpatient). Residential was more expensive, and I didn't believe she needed that. In my mind, all she did was use marijuana, which was absolutely not okay with me, but it wasn't as bad as cocaine or heroin. Surely, she would just need some counseling, and she'd be back on the right track in no time. The cost information we had included residential treatment, which is what Kyle recommended after speaking privately with Regan at their meeting. Since I wasn't there, I had to rely on her dad and his perception of both Pathway and Kyle.

Talking finances with my ex-husband was also not comfortable since this subject had been one he'd fought me on for years, complaining about paying child support. This whole thing required a lot of prayer on my part to trust that God had put us here not to leave us but to help us help our daughter.

I couldn't ask Tim to help with the cost of treatment for my daughter. He had already stepped in when I needed him most, helping me fight to keep my children years ago, and I still carried the weight of that. This was yet another mess, another crisis that he didn't deserve to be pulled into. He had signed up to be part of our family, yes—but not for this. Financially, we had always kept things separate. He covered the household bills while I managed everything for the kids with what I earned and the child support I received. And now, there was nothing left to pull from.

I loved my job managing a couple of family businesses from the same office, but I only worked thirty-two hours a week. The people I worked for were generous and good to me, but I couldn't ask for a raise to send my daughter to drug rehab. I hadn't even told anyone she was in Arizona. The thought of answering questions—of feeling the weight of their judgment, their assumptions, their whispered conversations behind my back—was unbearable. So far, she had been gone from her life here for almost three months, and not one person had even asked about her. Some days, that was a blessing. On other days, it was devastating. How could no one care that she had just disappeared?

Of course, my close friends and family knew, but that was a small circle. The rest of the world carried on as if nothing had happened while I lived in a fog of disbelief. How was this my life? How had we ended up here? I barely recognized my daughter anymore. Darkness had overtaken her, hollowing her out. This was not the life I had dreamed for her.

I prayed that God would make a way for me to pay my half of the cost of The Pathway Program. The math didn't work. No matter how many times I tried, the numbers never added up. So I quit trying to figure it out and just trusted Him. I had no other choice.

Before the weekend was over, I tried again to find other treatment options, this time focusing on Houston. I thought maybe it would be better for her to be closer to me, and that maybe I'd missed something in my previous searches. But I didn't find anything. It was disheartening to hang my hopes solely on this Pathway Program place. What if it didn't work out? I wanted to have a plan B, but there just wasn't one that was presenting itself, and I truly wasn't even sure I was looking for the right things. "Okay,

God," I thought, "Pathway it is." When I talked to Greg again, he deferred to me to make decisions and said he would support whatever I wanted to do. That felt terrifying, but at least there was no arguing.

Over the weekend, the plan became clearer. Regan had decided that she wanted to stay and enter the program, but would need to go back to her dad's to pack her things. She also needed to figure out what to do with Sofi since she couldn't take her to treatment. Her dad wasn't very excited to have Sofi there in the first place, but eventually agreed to take care of her temporarily while Regan went to Pathway. I would have gladly taken her, but getting her to Texas was going to be expensive, and nobody wanted to send Sofi on a plane alone.

Greg picked Regan up that Sunday, driving to get her after church and returning home with her by late afternoon. She took a shower, ate dinner, and decided to go see a movie with her dad. This was a nice change from three days prior!

The following morning, she packed up her clothes and necessities, stuffing everything into a duffel bag with little ceremony. There was no hesitation in her movements—no lingering glances around her room, no second-guessing what to bring. It was as if she had already detached from this part of her life, ready to move on from there.

Her dad loaded up the car, and they made the long drive back to Pathway to admit her into the program officially. I sat at my desk in Texas, my phone within reach, waiting for updates. My mind raced as I tried to grasp how quickly everything had unfolded. Just twelve days ago, she had been with me, home for spring break, and now we were making arrangements for her to live in a treatment center for the next six weeks. I felt like I was watching a movie on fast-forward, barely able to process one scene before being thrust into the next.

When Greg called me from the meeting with Kyle, we walked through the financial piece together. Thankfully, they offered a ten-month payment plan, which made it easier for me to manage. Still, the weight of it all settled heavily on my shoulders. She was definitely going into Step Two, even though I was still uncertain about it. But Greg made it clear that bringing her back home wasn't an option. The daily two-and-a-half-hour drive each way for outpatient treatment was unrealistic. She needed structure, stability, and daily accountability.

Step Two was the only choice.

She would move in the next day, sharing a house with up to seven other teens. Counseling sessions, daily group therapy, required meetings, and something called "functions" filled her schedule—most of which I didn't understand. I could only trust that they knew what they were doing. I told myself that this was what she needed, that they would help her, and that after six weeks, she would be back to normal.

There were no phones allowed in Step Two, so her phone went home with her dad that day. I had no way of contacting her except through her counselor, whom I had not met yet. I prayed for God to protect her and trusted that she was safe there. My sleep improved gradually, knowing this.

The next day, I didn't hear anything, but I figured no news was good news. She was officially in the program, so there was nothing left for me to do. Greg met Merrillee, her assigned counselor, when he dropped her off. She gave him a book to read for starters and encouraged him to return on Thursday for the parent meeting. Apparently, this meeting was just for parents and was every Thursday at 7 p.m. It wasn't required, but it was very strongly recommended. All the kids met at the same time in their respective groups. All of this was new to me, and so confusing.

When he returned for the meeting on Thursday, Greg saw both Regan and Merrillee. He reported that Regan was doing well and seemed happy, and Merrillee confirmed that she was adjusting well to her first couple of days.

The next day, I had my first phone call with Merrillee. My heart pounded as I answered, my mind racing with questions. I wanted answers—needed them—but more than anything, I needed her to know who my daughter really was. I wasn't just some mom in denial trying to paint my child in a better light. Regan was smart, funny, and kind. She was so much more than the mistakes she had made.

I launched into it—how special Regan was, how much I loved her, how this wasn't who she really was. My words tumbled out, one after another, as if I could just explain well enough, it might somehow change everything. Did I feel the need to tell her this so that she wouldn't think badly of her? Or of me? Maybe both.

Merrillee listened patiently, never rushing me, never cutting me off. When I finally paused to catch my breath, she responded in a way that surprised me—not with judgment, not with sympathy, but with steady reassurance. "She's doing fine," she told me. "This is a process, and she's right where she needs to be."

She explained that she would call me every Wednesday with updates, gave me the address to send letters and care packages, and promised to get them to Regan. The practical details grounded me for a moment, but when I hung up, I felt both relieved and completely lost. Only four days had passed, yet it felt like a lifetime.

Over the course of the six weeks Regan was in Step Two, I tried to find my way and determine what my role was in this new world. Pathway had so much structure and so many things to learn, even a new language. What is a wedge? (It's staying up all night.) I would ask Greg about the parent meetings to get a sense of what those were like, and my weekly talks with Merrillee became something I looked forward to. Early on, she let me know there had been something that Regan divulged to her that had been very difficult for her. She would not tell me what it was, but that they were working through it. Greg was called in for a meeting with both her and Regan. I couldn't ask Regan about it, and nobody told me then, but later, I found out that she had told Merrillee about being sexually abused by her dad's neighbor's teenage son when she was only four or five years old. This hit me like a gut punch. How did we never know about this? Why didn't she tell anyone? This was a conversation we would have a couple of months later.

Merrillee directed me to read a couple of books, *Beyond the Yellow Brick Road* and *Parent to Parent,* and suggested that I find an Al-Anon meeting to attend as soon as I could. The thought of sitting in a room full of strangers, admitting that my daughter was using drugs, and risking their judgment as a terrible parent felt impossible at that moment. I pushed it aside, choosing to focus on what I could handle for now. She ended up mailing me a copy of the *Yellow Brick Road* book, which I immediately read from cover to cover in one day. I couldn't put it down. It both intrigued me and completely terrified me. What is this world of teenagers and drugs and addiction and the twelve steps? It was so foreign to me. I had my husband read it and sent it to my mom as well. There was so much in that book that I needed those closest to me to understand with me. Maybe because it answered questions that I couldn't. I couldn't turn my brain off after finishing that book, and I didn't sleep much that night with it all whirling around in my head. Especially the chapters about parenting. My ex refused to co-parent our kids when they were growing up, and now we were reaping the consequences. It was all there in the book. I hoped he read it and felt it, too.

I made it a point to write Regan a letter each week she was in Step Two and send it with pictures I printed out and little gifts that I thought might brighten her day. I wanted her to know how loved she was. My letters were purposely written to avoid talking about her or asking her any questions about anything. I told her what was happening in my life, the things we were doing, and how much we loved and missed her. Merrillee would send me letters from Regan each week to my email. She would tell me how good she was doing, what she was learning, and how many days sober she had. Receiving her letters was the best, and I cherished every single word. But I never addressed anything she said. I wanted her experience to be all hers.

Eventually, I forced myself to attend an Al-Anon meeting on a Tuesday evening. It wasn't that I wanted to go—I just couldn't shake the feeling that if I didn't, I might somehow be failing Regan. Merrillee had suggested it to me since I was too far away to attend their parent meetings, and I was a rule follower. I didn't want my reluctance to be the thing that kept my daughter from getting better.

Even so, walking into that meeting felt like stepping into a world I didn't belong in. Wasn't this where the parents who had truly lost control ended up? The ones whose kids were beyond saving? I was still so uneducated about addiction and recovery, and I hated the idea that anyone might look at me and assume I had done something wrong—something that had led to this.

The people were kind and welcoming, but their stories felt foreign, their language unfamiliar. I didn't know how I fit into any of it or what I was supposed to say. The whole time, my heart pounded, and I couldn't wait to leave. I sat quietly, listening, absorbing bits and pieces of their experiences, but I walked out feeling just as lost as before. I knew I wouldn't go back.

On our next phone meeting the following week, I let Merrillee know, and she gave me a list of other Pathway moms whom I could connect with instead. This was extremely helpful to me. Over a week or two, I called each one of them and talked for hours—finally feeling like someone understood all the emotions and turmoil I was going through. I heard their stories, and they listened intently to mine. These moms also helped me acclimate to the Pathway Program, telling me what to expect, what the slang words all meant, and how nobody outside the program would understand it. They were all so *normal!* We all had lived a nightmare, but their kids were doing well, and it gave me something I really needed—*hope.*

REGAN

Dad picked me up from school, and we headed to this Pathway place. I refused to talk to him or even look in his direction for the entire two-hour drive. The silence felt heavy, but I didn't care. At one point, we stopped for gas, and he asked if I wanted anything from inside. I ignored him, staying in the car, arms crossed, staring out the window. The drive dragged on forever.

When we finally pulled up to Pathway, I was more than ready to get out of that car. A guy named Kyle greeted me and led me inside to talk. He introduced himself, but I wasn't interested in small talk. He asked me questions about my life, why I was there, and what was going on, but I barely answered. My default response to everything was, "I don't know."

Kyle didn't seem fazed. Instead of pushing, he switched tactics.

"Why don't I start by telling you what I've been through and why I'm here?"

That got my attention.

I sat back and listened as he told me his story—how he had been into drugs, how his life had spiraled, and how he had gone through The Pathway Program himself before becoming a counselor. That opened me up a little, but I still wasn't giving him much. Then he started asking about drugs.

"Have you ever smoked weed?"

"I don't know."

"Have you ever tried anything else? Acid? Coke?"

"I don't know."

He kept listing them, and eventually, I admitted I may have done *some* of that stuff.

After our talk, Kyle met with Dad while I waited in the lobby. I was sitting there, minding my own business, when suddenly a bunch of kids came in, immediately striking up conversations with me. I had no idea who they were, but they acted like they'd known me forever. I was so annoyed.

Three girls in particular sat around me, throwing questions at me, trying to get me to talk. I answered in short sentences, hoping they'd get the hint, but they kept at it. One of them mentioned something about going to get Dutch, and I had no idea what she was talking about.

"What's Dutch?" I asked.

Their jaws dropped. "You've never had Dutch Bros?!"

"No?"

"Oh, we *have* to take you," one of them said. "You're coming with us."

At this point, I didn't care what we did as long as it got me away from my dad. Kyle had invited us to stay for a meeting that night anyway, so I figured I might as well check the place out.

One of the girls drove us to Dutch Bros, and they were all talking a mile a minute, asking what kind of drinks I liked. I had no idea, so Becca, one of the girls, told me I could just get what she got.

"They have energy drinks, and you can pick flavors to mix with them," she explained.

Sounded fine to me. When we got to the drive-thru, I ordered the exact same thing as her—a large iced Rebel with pomegranate, passion fruit, and mango. They even paid for it.

And honestly? It was really good.

We went back to Pathway, though I don't remember much about the meeting itself—I just know we stayed for it. By the time it ended, it was dark outside, and the last thing I wanted was to go back home with Dad. Just thinking about it made my stomach turn.

Then, the girls came to my rescue. "Hey, do you wanna spend the night with us?" one of them asked.

I shrugged, but my answer didn't really matter—I wasn't going to be the one asking. "You'll have to talk to *him*," I said, pointing over at my dad. "I'm not speaking to him."

I stood back and watched as this group of teenage girls *swarmed* him, all talking at once. He looked *terrified*. I could just imagine them ganging up on him, begging, pleading, overwhelming him with their energy. I saw him nod, and the girls turned back to me, all grins and excitement.

"You can stay!"

Dad walked over to me a minute later, looking unsure. "Would you, uh… want to stay the night with them?"

"Yeah," I said flatly.

"Okay, well… I'm gonna go ahead and head home then."

"Bye." That was all I gave him. No emotion, no hesitation. I just wanted him gone.

And when he finally left, I felt nothing but relief.

It ended up being more than just one night—I stayed the entire weekend. We crashed at Ella's house (one of the girls in this group), went to Dutch Bros again, and hung out at all their usual spots. Even though I enjoyed it, part of me still thought, *These people are so gullible.* I had zero intention of changing. For months, my plan had been simple: either die or turn eighteen, cut everybody off, and disappear. That was *the dream.* No more pain, no more fake relationships, no more people lying to me, using me, or pretending to care.

And yet, there was something about these girls. I didn't want to like them, but I did. I didn't want to feel like maybe, just maybe, there was still something good out there, but the thought crept in anyway. I still planned to keep using. Nothing had changed in that regard. But it would be nice to have friends like this. If I let myself. I decided I would just play along for now—smile, act nice, do what I needed to do until I figured out what came next.

Dad picked me up on Sunday, but I barely remember anything about it. What I *do* remember is Tuesday, when I packed up my stuff and went to start Step Two.

Step Two was the residential treatment program, but before I could go, I had to do IOP (Intensive Outpatient) first. When I got there, a female staff member took me into an office and made me do a strip search. They also went through every single one of my bags to make sure I wasn't bringing anything in.

It felt *very* prison-like.

After that, they brought me into the IOP group just long enough for introductions. A few kids said their names, and I muttered mine, but before I even had time to sit down and figure out what the hell was going on, they called me back out.

"That was your IOP," they told me. "Now it's time to go to Step Two."

Wait… *what?*

The next thing I knew, I was being shuffled outside and put into this *really* crappy van with a bunch of kids I didn't know. I wasn't talking to anybody, and they stuck me in the front seat because I was new. I just stared out the window, trying to process what was happening, when I heard the driver's voice.

His name was Looter, and apparently, he had one goal: to make me laugh. The entire drive, he kept cracking jokes, making weird faces, and doing everything he could to get a reaction out of me. I fought it at first, keeping my expression blank, but it felt like I had stepped into some kind of alternate reality.

What *was* this place? And who *were* these people?

I picked up on the rules, routines, and schedules pretty fast. They didn't waste any time throwing me into it. We barely had enough time to do quick introductions and unpack before we were already heading back out for a meeting. Meetings were every single day in Step Two.

That first night, after we got back, we all sat on the porch and talked for a long time. Well, *they* talked. I mostly just listened. I wasn't about to start sharing my life story with a bunch of strangers, so I gave them the bare minimum—my name, and that was about it.

The first week in Step Two was easy. Everybody was welcoming, constantly telling me they loved me, giving me hugs, making it seem like this was some big, happy family. Merrillee, our counselor, was brutal—but not to me. I watched her absolutely roast everybody else in the group, but she didn't say a word to me. I thought, *Wow. These people are all kinds of messed up.* Since she wasn't calling me out, I figured I must be fine. I kept quiet, stayed in my corner at the other end of the table, and thought, *Maybe this place won't be so bad.*

One of the best things about Step Two was not having a phone. I didn't have to worry about texts, calls, or checking social media—none of it. It was actually kind of refreshing. The house itself was simple, nothing special, and the only entertainment we had was this old, crappy radio. Then there was the van. *That* thing was straight out of a kidnapping PSA—an old, gray, middle-aged creeper van with no working seatbelts and a barely functioning radio. It looked like it hadn't been updated since the 1980s.

But honestly, what I enjoyed the most was finally being away from my life. Those first few weeks, just learning the ropes, almost felt like being high. Not in the literal sense, but in the way that I wasn't *me* anymore. I was somewhere new, around people who didn't know me, didn't know my past, and didn't have any expectations of me. It was like I had stepped into a completely different reality, and for the first time in a long time, I didn't have to deal with my family, my problems, or my pain.

After the first week, the counselors started actually talking to me about my problems. I tried not to give them much—I didn't want to. Merrillee started off pretty easy, just asking questions about what led me here and what my life had been like. Eventually, I opened up and told them my whole story—all the things I'd been through.

When I first did my intake with Merrillee, I hadn't been entirely honest about everything I was struggling with. It took me at least a week to start feeling like I could trust them—to believe that they weren't just going to stab me in the back like I was used to. At some point, after a group session, I went back to Merrillee and admitted that I hadn't told her everything. That's when I finally said it out loud for the first time—I told her about the sexual abuse I'd experienced when I was four and five years old. She was the first person I ever told.

I admitted that I didn't even know how it had affected me. I was so young that I didn't know what emotions I had about it, if any. I just knew I had never told anyone before. I remember telling her I felt bad for lying to her, for keeping that to myself. She was really sweet about it, really kind. She told me she appreciated me telling her, and then she gave me a hug.

That night back at the house, I actually felt good. For the first time in a long time, it felt like maybe someone was really on my side.

That feeling didn't last long.

Merrillee started pushing me harder, trying to get me to talk about my pain, and I wasn't budging. I hated everybody. I blamed everyone in my life for my actions, including my drug use. No part of me felt like it was my fault, no matter how many times she told me that we're all in charge of our own choices. She kept saying that nobody made me do anything, that I was the one who chose my actions—and that I had chosen poorly. But I wasn't going to fight with her about it because I didn't care. As far as I was concerned, I was justified. After everything I had been through, after being lied to my whole life and treated like I didn't matter, how could she expect me to just take responsibility?

She wouldn't accept my answers, no matter what I said.

Sarcastically, I threw her a bone. "Okay, yeah, I guess I'm sorry for screaming at my dad."

I wasn't. She knew it.

But I wasn't just not sorry for yelling. I wasn't sorry for doing drugs, either. Even if my actions weren't the best, I hadn't caused them even a fraction of the pain they had caused me. So no, I wasn't sorry—and I think that shocked her.

The whole room went silent.

She kept looking at me, waiting, expecting me to crack. But she couldn't convince me to feel bad because I just didn't. I had spent my whole life trying to love my family, trying to have relationships with them, and all it ever got me was being pulled in every direction, put in the middle, yelled at, and blamed for things that weren't my fault. I didn't care if I had hurt them because my choices weren't about them. My drug use wasn't about them. It was about me.

I didn't even understand how it affected them. It's my life, not theirs.

Boy, did I have a rude awakening.

Merrillee didn't appreciate that conversation one bit.

A few days later, she tried a different approach. We were in IOP, and again, she came for me, asking the same d*** questions. Again, I refused to budge. She wasn't going to get to me, and she wasn't going to make me feel bad. I was too angry. Nobody seemed to understand that my whole life had been nothing but listening to the same stories from my parents—except each time, they were flipped, making the other parent the villain. Or worse, the stories didn't match at all, like they were living in two completely different realities.

How could I trust either of them? How could I trust anyone? I hated them for it. I hated the lies. I hated the pain. And I hated that nobody saw how much it had messed me up.

Merrillee must have known she wasn't getting through to me because she got really quiet. The whole room went still.

And then, she looked right at me and said, **"You know, for all the s*** you talk about how horrible your dad and your mom are, you're turning out just like them."**

Instantly, I was broken. The second she said it, the tears started, and they didn't stop. I cried through the lunch break, through the entire hour. I cried on the van ride to the meeting that night, then sat in the bathroom sobbing for most of it. On the way back, I kept my face turned toward the window, trying to hold myself together, but it was useless. As soon as we got home, I went straight to my room, lay on my bed, and cried into my pillow.

The girls came in and asked me to come to the living room with them. They didn't want me to be alone. I didn't want to be alone either, but I didn't know how to face anyone. Still, I went.

I sat there, curled up, while silent tears kept falling. Nobody spoke a word. Two of the girls sat beside me on the couch while the rest—including the staff—sat on the floor around me, like it was storytime or something. Two new kids had just moved into the house that day, and this was what they were walking into. They probably didn't even know my name yet. But they sat there with me anyway.

I could not stop crying. I don't think I'd ever cried that hard in my entire life. Hours passed. It wasn't until sometime after 3 a.m. that I finally managed to choke out words. Through my tears, I told them everything. Every horrible thing I'd ever done, everything that had ever happened to me, everything I had buried deep and never spoken aloud.

And instead of judging me, they just *sat with me*. Nobody got up to get food, shower, or head to bed. Nobody told me I was too much or tried to make it better. **They just stayed.**

For the first time in my life, I felt completely, unconditionally loved.

That night, something shifted. I had planned to leave. I had been counting down the days, waiting until I could get out and get high again. But now? That didn't seem so appealing anymore. I thought, *maybe I actually want to give this a shot. Maybe I do want to try to get better.*

That was the night my entire world changed.

Not long after that, a girl named Kate showed up. She became my best friend almost instantly. We bonded over our shared distrust of girls, both of us having been burned by friendships before. At first, neither of us was sure about letting the other in. But once we did, we were inseparable.

Kate had an iPod Nano that we could hook up to the ancient, broken-down kidnapper van. That changed our lives. Finally, we could play actual music instead of suffering through static-filled radio stations.

As some of the other girls moved out, I switched rooms and moved in with Kate. We pushed our beds together and made that room ours. Every night, we talked and laughed until we fell asleep. I hadn't had that kind of connection with someone in a long time.

Leaving Step Two was harder than I expected. I hated it. The close friendships I had built were with the Step Two people, but most of them—including Kate—went back home to cities closer to where they lived.

It felt like I had to start over. Again.

I begged to stay in Step Two a little longer, and they let me stay an extra few days. But I would've stayed there forever if I could have.

Chapter 8
S.O.

Toward the end of Step Two, each kid was required to invite their family members to what they called an "S.O.", which stands for "Significant Other." This meeting was for the purpose of the person in treatment to make amends to their loved ones before graduating and moving on to outpatient treatment. Regan's S.O. was scheduled for May 7th. She had a separate S.O. with her dad and brother prior to the one Tim and I went to, further bringing attention to the extreme brokenness of her family. While I had been informed about what to expect at this meeting by the other moms who had experienced it before me, it all felt really strange. I still felt like I didn't know what would happen, but I was super excited to finally see Regan again after everything that had happened since I last got to hug her.

We headed to Phoenix a couple of days prior to the S.O., which was on a Monday afternoon. Spending the weekend in the same city as my daughter but not seeing her felt strange and unnatural, another reminder of how much things had changed. That weekend, we had dinner with the four moms I'd only spoken to over the phone in the previous weeks. Sitting across from them in person, I expected to feel like an outsider—ashamed, uncertain, and fearful of what lay ahead. Instead, they welcomed me instantly, their warmth dissolving my anxiety. They spoke candidly about their own experiences, sharing both heartbreak and hope in a way that was somehow reassuring. I asked questions about Pathway, their kids, and the S.O. They answered openly, without judgment or hesitation.

One of the moms, Lori, asked if I had been to a parent meeting yet. When I admitted I hadn't, she immediately offered to call me in on Thursday nights so I could be part of them from home. It was such a simple gesture, yet it felt like a lifeline. I eagerly accepted, grateful beyond words, for the support of these women who had once stood exactly where I was.

Before we left, Lori also invited Tim and me to lunch the next day with her daughter. The restaurant they picked? Rehab Burger Therapy. As we pulled up, Lori laughed and asked, "Too soon?" But honestly, it wasn't. I still had my sense of humor, and I knew she just wanted to lighten the mood—to remind me that this road, though painful, didn't have to be all darkness. I appreciated that more than she knew.

The day finally arrived, and we met with Josh, the owner of Pathway, at the Step Two house toward late afternoon. I liked him, but he made me nervous. He was kind and a bit business-like, but had really nice things to say about Regan. He let us know that after the meeting, we were free to take Regan with us to have dinner and spend time with her as long as she was back at the house by 9 p.m. Then he walked us over to the house, which was a fairly nondescript mobile home, and led us into the living room. The place was decent and cared for, definitely not fancy, but livable. The furniture was positioned around the room in a circle, and we sat down on one end. We didn't see Regan, but several other kids came in and sat down around us, chatting, laughing, and introducing themselves to us. Merrilee met with us as well earlier that day to tell us what to expect and gave us a progress note she'd written, along with her completion paperwork for Step Two. She greeted us warmly at the house and then went to get Regan.

When she entered the room, my heart pounded in my chest, a mix of anticipation and curiosity swelling inside me. My eyes instantly welled with tears, blurring my vision as I took her in. She looked good—healthy, even. Her very short hair was covered with a scarf-like covering, her face was clear, and she had light in her eyes. And then she smiled, and I let out a breath I didn't even realize I had been holding. A real, genuine, happy-to-see-us smile. That small moment, that simple expression, cracked something open in me. Maybe she was going to be okay.

She sat on the side of the room facing us. Her closest friends in the group spoke first, sharing how much she had changed since starting Step Two. They described the girl they met when she first arrived—guarded, angry, lost—and how, little by little, she softened, let people in, and fought for something better. I listened, taking it all in, feeling both gratitude and heartbreak. Gratitude that she was here, safe, surrounded by people who saw the good in her. Heartbreak that she had needed to fight so hard to find her way back.

Then, it was her turn. She took a shaky breath, looking down at the paper in her hands, then up at us. She addressed Tim first, confessing the ways she had lied to him, manipulated him, and stolen from us both. Her voice trembled, but she kept going. Then she turned to me, and our eyes met. Tears spilled down her cheeks as she admitted how deeply she had hurt me, how her actions had betrayed my trust, and taken a toll on our relationship. Didn't she know that none of that even mattered to me? That I would have walked through fire for her, no matter what? My heart ached to reach for her, to pull her into my arms, but I didn't dare move. This was her moment, and she had to finish. So I smiled at her through my own tears, hoping she could see and feel everything I couldn't say just yet—I love you, I forgive you, you are still my girl.

When she was done, Tim responded. His voice was steady at first, but quickly gave way to teary emotion. His words were kind and loving, and my heart swelled when I saw how much he loved and cared about her. Tears fell down Regan's cheeks instantly as she listened to his words.

Then it was my turn. I kept it short and simple but made sure she heard what mattered most.

"I appreciate you telling us all of this," I told her gently, "but there is nothing you could ever do to make me love you any less." She smiled through tears as the weight of my words settled over her. It was a moment I would never forget. Awkward, yes—but also raw, beautiful, and healing in a way I hadn't known we all needed.

It all took maybe thirty minutes in total—the build-up far exceeded the actual experience. But it was something that would stick with me far into the future. When we finally got to embrace her, I didn't want to let go, but I also couldn't wait to talk to her. The rest of the evening flew by in a blur of laughter and easy conversation. We took her to a sushi restaurant where the plates traveled past on a conveyor belt—something I had never seen before. She had fun explaining how it worked while I marveled at the tiny plates rolling by, still a little distracted by the surreal nature of the night. After dinner, we wandered through the mall, stopping in random stores and chatting about everything and nothing.

At some point, we spotted a photo booth tucked into a corner. Without hesitation, we crammed inside, making silly faces and laughing as we tried to time our expressions before the flash went off. When the strip of pictures printed, Regan giggled, holding them up for us to see—our three faces squished together, and Tim making googly eyes. It felt so normal.

When we pulled up to the Step Two house later that night to drop her off, the bittersweetness settled in. I didn't want to leave her, but I did so with more peace and hope than I had felt in a long time.

She graduated from Step Two and started intensive outpatient (IOP) over the next few days. She was happy to have her phone returned to her and promptly sat down with her sponsor to go through and delete everyone she needed to have contact with no longer. There were friends she texted goodbye to and others she just deleted. Her sponsor was over a year sober, and she would end up staying with her and her family for the duration of IOP, which was a minimum of eight weeks. My first text message from Regan was on Mother's Day, the Sunday after her S.O. It read:

> Happy Mother's Day Gorgeous, I love you so so much!!

Greg and I determined how much of an allowance we would provide for Regan during her time there and discussed whether she should have her car or not. We decided to wait on the car for a while, but since she would need money for the group's weekly functions (fun events) on Fridays and Saturdays, we came up with giving her $70 each week. This was to cover her functions and any food or other items she might need. That worked for a while, but we ended up increasing it because she was always out of money. She struggled to get rides to OP every day for about three weeks before finally convincing us she needed her car. These were difficult decisions to make, and we included Kyle (who was known as Boomer to us as well at that point) in making them. Only with his blessing would we be okay with letting her have her car. A priority for us was to be a united front, as the program encouraged parents to be. We worked to make decisions together, and any changes would be made together as well.

One of the hardest things for me during this time was seeing all of her classmates and friends here graduating from high school and making college plans. The prom pictures and the graduation party photos were everywhere on social media for what felt like weeks. While I was truly happy for these families and friends, I struggled with not getting to experience these memorable events with my own daughter. Each photo I saw felt like a gut punch—a reminder of what was taken from me, of the hopes and dreams I had carried for years that would never come to be.

I had pictured those moments so vividly—the dress shopping, the cap-and-gown photos, the teary-eyed joy of watching her walk across the stage. I had envisioned the pride of sending out graduation announcements, planning a celebration in her honor, and taking pictures together to commemorate the milestone. But none of it would happen, at least not in the way I had always imagined. Instead, I found myself mourning something that had never even existed outside of my own heart.

The grief was unexpected, but it was real. I found myself withdrawing, avoiding conversations about college visits and senior celebrations. I gave myself permission to mute and snooze friends on social media temporarily for thirty days—not because I wasn't happy for them, but because I couldn't handle the constant reminders of what I had lost. Looking back, I realize it was my way of taking care of myself, of protecting my heart, while I tried to recalibrate my reality.

I had to come to terms with the fact that these dreams had been mine, not hers. And as much as it hurt, I had to let them go.

My first weekend visit to see Regan was in mid-June, and thanks to another mom in the program, we had a vacant home to stay in for the weekend. The privacy gave us a rare opportunity to be alone together, uninterrupted, for the first time in months. Though she still attended her group functions in the evenings, our days were completely ours.

She was excited to introduce me to Dutch Bros, which I quickly realized was more than just a coffee shop—it was an experience. The drive-thru was alive with energy, with loud dance music blasting through the speakers and employees who acted as if they'd been waiting all day just for us. I loved it as much as she did, and we went every morning during my visit.

On Saturday, we spent the entire day in the arts district of Phoenix, walking through the maze of murals that colored the city in bold, vibrant strokes. Regan's hair was still short, but it had grown out enough that she no longer covered it with scarves and hats. She looked more like herself—girly and open to wearing clothes that didn't swallow her whole or make her look like she was homeless. I snapped pictures of her in front of the murals, capturing the moment, wanting to remember it exactly as it was. It was blistering hot, and we were both sweating as we wandered through the streets, but neither of us minded that much. The conversation flowed easily, laughter weaving its way through our words like it always had.

But then, in the quiet of her car, the conversation shifted. I don't know what made me ask, but before she drove us to find dinner, I found myself looking over at her and finally saying the words that had been sitting on my chest for weeks. "What happened in those first few weeks at Step Two?"

She hesitated for a moment, her fingers tightening slightly around the steering wheel. "You don't know?" she asked, glancing at me.

I shook my head. "No one told me."

And then, she did.

She told me about the abuse she had endured. The words hung heavy in the air between us, filling every space in the car. I felt my breath hitch, my stomach twisting into knots. My mind reeled, trying to process what she was saying, trying to absorb the weight of it. How had this happened? Why hadn't she told me? Had she been carrying this alone all this time?

We talked—really talked—for the first time in what felt like forever. She asked questions about my choices, my relationship with her dad, my struggles with Jacob, and why things had played out the way they did. And I asked her about her drug use, about what she had been thinking during those dark days, about the pain she had been holding onto. There were things she told me that day that I never knew, and vice versa. We laughed and we cried, but mostly, we bonded. It was a time when both of us were able to start piecing together our experiences like putting together a puzzle, with the missing pieces finally put into place.

Our relationship was forever going to be different as we gained this new understanding of one another. It was a long-overdue conversation and a pivotal moment in my life as a mom.

I'd been phoning into the Thursday night parent meetings for several weeks, soaking up all that I could. There was always talk about finding a sponsor and working through the Twelve Steps at the beginning of each meeting, yet it seemed that few parents were interested. Around the time I went to visit Regan for the first time,

I decided to get a sponsor and do the steps in order to be able to talk to her about what she was learning. It became really important to me to support her in the best way possible, so I needed to know what it was all about.

One of the moms whom I met at dinner in May agreed to sponsor me, and we got straight to work. She sent me a workbook in my email and guided me through each step, giving me time to complete the homework and acting as my accountability partner as we discussed my work and applied it to my daily living. Quickly, I realized the value of the Twelve Steps and wondered why they aren't taught in every school in the country. Instead of just working on the steps to better support Regan, I ended up using them to change my own life for the better.

Having Regan in Phoenix while I was in Texas and her dad was two and a half hours away made everything feel complicated and uncertain. As her time in IOP was winding down in early July, the looming question of where she would live during aftercare weighed heavily on all of us. The next phase of treatment would last six months, but the structure she had relied on was about to shift dramatically—no more daily group meetings, only regular check-ins with her counselor. This was a huge transition, and I knew how fragile transitions could be. We had been warned: this was the time many kids struggled, when the safety net of a rigid schedule was removed, and real-life responsibilities began pressing in.

Ultimately, we wanted Regan to start taking ownership of her life, so we left the decision largely up to her. She needed to find a stable living situation that would allow her to stay connected with Pathway while also giving her the independence she would need to continue growing. A friend of mine knew a couple in the Phoenix area and offered to reach out to them. While Regan met them and liked them, their home wasn't close to where she spent most of her time, making it an impractical option.

Meanwhile, Boomer was helping set expectations for this next chapter so we wouldn't have to navigate everything on our own. He encouraged her to enroll in an alternative school nearby to finish high school and find a job to support herself. Both her dad and I felt it was time to end the weekly allowance she had been receiving, hoping this would push her to take more financial responsibility. Things were going well—she was maintaining her sobriety, being deeply involved in Pathway, and staying active in meetings and events. We pushed her to do more at this time without realizing that it might be too much all at once.

Regan had found a place to stay with another family in the program whose daughter was a few years younger. They had rules for their home that she had to agree to abide by, but they were very invested and active at Pathway. Right about the time she moved in, I woke up on a Sunday morning early to a voicemail from Boomer on my phone from the night before. This was never a good thing. My heart raced as I listened to his voice tell me that she had left a function early last night, which was against the rules. He also said she'd been hanging out with a couple of other kids who seemed to be "up to no good" the night before, and she was a part of it. He asked me to call him back. I checked the time; it had been about four hours since he left me the message. Where was she? Was she okay? Had she relapsed? I tried calling Boomer and got his voicemail. Then I called and texted my daughter in a panic. I felt like I was going to throw up.

It was July 15th, she was almost four months sober, and I had made plans to attend a new church that morning. I had a few hours to get this figured out before needing to look presentable and make it to the service on time. It was 4:53 a.m. in Arizona when I texted Regan to "call me immediately, please." An hour and a half went by. I had called her multiple times with no answer. I texted again, simply, "Call me." She finally did. She sounded fine and reassured me that she was fine, but admitted that she had considered relapsing the night before. Transitioning out of OP was difficult for her, and she felt the strain of the expectations everyone had of her now. She knew she was in trouble with Boomer, and we had to have a meeting to discuss her path forward and whether she would be allowed to remain in the group after breaking the rules. When the family she'd been staying with found out what had happened, they decided they didn't want her to live with them anymore. I felt defeated and terrified for my daughter. I forced myself to go to church, but I arrived late, and it took me time to finish telling Greg what had transpired before I willed myself to get out of the car and go inside.

I wanted to go back home and get back in bed. It was all too much for me. I found a seat somewhere in the middle of the room, hoping to be invisible as the praise team was already singing worship songs. I looked up to find two huge wooden walls that were pieced together with multiple two-by-fours in a variety of colors of wood. The center was cut out in the shape of a cross. These instantly reminded me of the wall that was behind Regan in so many of the pictures she'd sent me of herself during group at Pathway. I loved that wall and had often asked her where it was, and she would say, "It's at the shop," which is what they called the place at Pathway where they had their meetings and hung out all the time. The striking similarity unraveled me, and before I could stop them, tears welled up and spilled down my cheeks. The music swelled around me, but I was no longer fully present in the room. My heart pounded, my chest tightening under the weight of everything I had been holding inside. The fear. The exhaustion. The helplessness. But in that moment, something shifted.

A warmth spread through my chest, a quiet but firm reassurance, as if God was gently pressing His presence into my soul. And then, clear as day, I heard it—not an audible voice, but something deeper, something undeniable: *I am there with her.* The words echoed inside me, wrapping around my heart and steadying my breath. I didn't need to hold it all together. I didn't need to have all the answers. He was with her, and I didn't have to carry this burden alone.

I honestly couldn't recall a single thing the pastor said that day. It didn't matter. What mattered was that I walked out of that church lighter than I had felt in months, filled with something I hadn't allowed myself to fully embrace in a long time—relief. God had her. God had me. And somehow, I knew we were going to be okay.

We met with Boomer on Monday late afternoon, Regan, her dad, and him in the room with me on speakerphone. It felt a bit like being in the principal's office, only he was much younger than us. Regan apologized for leaving the function early and said she was afraid she was going to be kicked out of Pathway because of her actions. Boomer was gracious in giving her another chance to stay and asked if she would be interested in helping out with the newcomers. We also discussed keeping her accountable with the Life360 app so we could see her location at all times. Overall, Regan promised she would keep us informed of where she was and what she was doing and that she would stick with winners in the program. A "winner" is a person who is sober and working on a recovery program. I felt relieved that this meeting went well and that Regan seemed to be back on track.

I returned for another visit for Regan's eighteenth birthday in September. She was staying with a family who lived a ways from Pathway, but they had an extra bedroom and let her land there when she needed a place to sleep, do her laundry, and have some privacy. When I visited, I was invited to stay there for the weekend, too. I arrived on Thursday in time to attend the parent meeting in person for the first time. There was a lot I missed being on speakerphone! I also met many of the kids, especially Regan's friends, who were all so friendly and welcoming. Being there made me love the place even more.

Of course, we made our daily stop at Dutch Bros and spent time at the mall because she needed new clothes. I struck a deal with her—I'd buy her some new outfits if she agreed to clean out her old, baggy, drab "homeless clothes" and throw them away. To my relief, she didn't hesitate. After picking out several pieces she loved at the mall, we went back to her room, stuffed a garbage bag full of her old wardrobe, and tossed it into a dumpster. She didn't complain, and I felt victorious, saying goodbye to what reminded me of her darkest days.

The group had a birthday party for her and another girl that I got to attend. Seeing her turn eighteen was a big deal because she shared with me that she never thought she would live to be eighteen. Her plan was to die from using drugs by then. Writing that still makes me feel like I can't breathe.

Now that she was eighteen, it became even more important to her dad and me that she find a job and finish high school. She finally agreed to enroll in the credit recovery program that many other Pathway kids had attended, a safer alternative to returning to their old schools and falling back in with old friends. She wasn't thrilled about it, though, and her effort reflected that.

Finding a job was another hurdle, but she eventually found a couple of nannying jobs that kept her busy during the daytime and gave her money to spend.

As I continued participating in the parent meetings and learning more about recovery, it became more important to support Regan's sobriety than to put too many other requirements on her. After all, without being sober, none of the other stuff mattered anyway. Her dad had stopped going to the meetings by the end of the summer, but he was agreeable to my suggestions about how to set boundaries while supporting her recovery process.

My relationship with Regan continued to grow and evolve during this time. Despite my near-constant worry about her staying sober and moving forward with her life, she kept in regular contact with me, and we had really nice talks about her life, her friends, and what she was experiencing. While I found Life360 a cool idea at the outset, I quickly discovered it made me more neurotic seeing her location twenty-four-seven, especially when I'd check it in the middle of the night and see her driving around. I was unfamiliar with Phoenix, so I never knew where she was or whether she was somewhere she shouldn't be, not to mention who she was with. The app was not helpful for me overall, and I suggested to her and her dad that we stop using it. She was patient with me when I'd call her at odd hours to ask her where she was and what she was doing, but I knew this behavior was very unhealthy on my part. What was I going to do if she was somewhere she shouldn't be? I was all the way in Texas! Besides, she was in control of her decisions, not me. If she was going to relapse, there wasn't anything I could do to prevent it. This was something I had to remind myself of continually.

In November, when I visited Regan for the last time in Phoenix, she had landed at her friend Ella's home—a family that could only be described as a Godsend. They all but adopted her as their own, ensuring she was well-fed and had everything she needed. Mama Maureen was a gift—kind, wise, and nurturing. She regularly engaged Regan in long, heartfelt conversations, fostering a close relationship that brought my daughter a sense of safety and belonging that had been absent for far too long. When I arrived, they welcomed me just as warmly, opening their home as if I were family, and I shared a bedroom with the girls. Regan's hair had grown back several inches—now a light, platinum blonde that framed her face at her jawline. She looked fantastic, and more importantly, she felt more feminine with longer hair.

As we always did when I visited, we went to the mall for an afternoon of shopping. We were strolling through when a saleswoman at a kiosk called us over, offering to let Regan try on clip-in hair extensions. She eagerly agreed and couldn't sit down fast enough. As the woman began fastening the long blonde strands into Regan's hair, I watched my daughter's expression shift. The excitement in her eyes was replaced by something deeper, something raw. Her fingers trembled as she reached up, brushing the soft waves cascading down her shoulders. And then, the tears came—silent at first, slipping down her cheeks through the biggest smile I'd seen in a long time.

I felt my throat tighten. She had always loved her long hair. Watching her now, seeing how much she had longed for this, I suddenly understood what I had failed to see before. Cutting off all her hair hadn't just been an impulsive decision—it had been a scream for help, a severing of the person she no longer wanted to be, or maybe the person she thought she could never be again. We had thought it was just hair. But it wasn't.

The saleswoman continued curling the extensions, seamlessly blending them into Regan's real hair. The transformation was stunning. I pulled out my phone and snapped picture after picture, wanting to capture this moment—her radiant smile, her sparkling eyes, the way she held herself with confidence. She looked beautiful. She felt beautiful. And then, the realization hit—she would have to take them out before we left.

The instant the woman started unclipping the pieces, Regan's face crumpled. Joy drained from her eyes, and fresh tears spilled over. I felt my own chest tighten. She wasn't ready to let go of this feeling again. Seeing her reaction, the saleswoman hesitated, emotion welling up in her eyes. She placed a hand over her heart and said, "She needs these." All three of us were crying now.

I nodded, already knowing there was no way we were leaving without them. The woman offered us a huge discount, saying she just wanted Regan to have them and that she wished she could give them to her for free. It wasn't just about the extensions—it was about giving her back something she had lost, something she was desperately trying to reclaim.

As we walked away, her fingers continuously ran through her hair as if she still couldn't believe it. She couldn't wait to show her friends what she looked like with long hair. I told her she looked beautiful. And she did. But more than that, she looked like a girl finding herself again. And that was the most beautiful thing I had ever seen.

REGAN

I didn't feel like I should even have to do an S.O. I never really felt like I had anything to apologize to my family for. Apologizing for using drugs felt ridiculous compared to everything else that had happened in my life. In my mind, they were definitely not the wronged party. I worked hard at convincing my counselors that I didn't need to do one, and they almost relented, but in the end, they decided I had to.

I chose to do separate S.O.s—one for Mom and Tim and one for my dad and Jacob—because there was no way all of us could sit in one room together and then spend the rest of the evening pretending everything was fine. That was never going to happen. Honestly, I thought it was completely pointless to even do one for my dad and Jacob after the way they had treated me for years. But I did it anyway. I don't remember many details about my S.O. with Mom and Tim, other than that, we went to a sushi restaurant for dinner and took photos in the photo booth at the mall.

When I officially completed Step Two, I got my phone back—sort of. It actually went to my sponsor first. Her job was to go through it and delete anyone she deemed wasn't a "winner" for me. I wasn't thrilled about that. Honestly, I would have preferred to just stay in Step Two and not have my phone at all, but once I was out, it was nice to have it. What I didn't like was my sponsor having free rein over my contacts. I begged her to please keep Olivia's number, even though it didn't really make sense. I hadn't talked to Olivia since the afternoon at the lake park before I left for Arizona, but for some reason, it was really important to me to keep her number.

Then came the part I hated the most—texting the few close friends I had left to tell them I couldn't be their friend anymore. The hardest one was Sara. I still cared about her, and I knew the message was going to hurt her. She texted back, saying she was also trying to get clean and was happy for me, but she really wanted to stay friends. We went back and forth a few times, and she pleaded with me to stay in her life. But in the end, I had to tell her goodbye. I hated that I did that to her.

The transition from Step Two to IOP (intensive outpatient) was really hard. In Step Two, I finally had stability. I had people who felt like family, and I truly didn't want to leave the place where I felt safe and loved. Moving into outpatient felt like my security was being ripped away again. On top of that, I realized I didn't really know anyone in the outpatient group because I had spent all my time with the Step Two kids. I didn't want to start over and make new friendships, but over time, I got to know some of the other kids. Still, nobody ever replaced the family I had in Step Two.

What made it even harder was watching all eight of my closest friends finish their time in residential treatment and go back to their home states. One by one, they left, and every time, it broke my heart.

I loved it when Mom came to visit, but I felt torn between my life there and spending time with her. I took her to Dutch and made sure they put sparkles in our drinks because I knew she'd love that. We went to the mall, and I liked getting nicer clothes, but at the same time, I hated missing out on all the hangouts with my friends. It made me happy that I could do both, and it didn't seem to bother Mom when I left to go do my sober, fun activities. She was just glad I was happy.

On that first visit, we had a really long talk in my car. I don't remember all the specifics, but I remember how it felt—like a wall finally coming down between us.

Toward the end of outpatient, I started having a rough time. I was about to transition again—out of outpatient and into after-care—and I was also about to turn eighteen. That meant I'd be moving from the younger group (seventeen and under) to the older group (eighteen and over). I wasn't ready for any of it.

The night I left the function early, I was planning to relapse. I had been about four months sober, but I was still struggling mentally. Allie, one of my good friends in the group, had started dating Cameron, a chronic relapser also in the group. That night, they were together, getting high. I called Allie from the function, and she invited me to come over. On my way there, I stopped at another kid's house—someone who used to be in the group but wasn't anymore.

When I got there, he was smoking in the backyard, and I sat across from him. His bong was right between us. He started questioning me about why I wanted to use and whether I planned to stay in the Pathway group or leave. He told me that if I really, really wanted to smoke, I could—but he wanted me to be sure that was what I actually wanted.

Talking to him, I felt like I was talking to Boomer. Something about it got to me, and I changed my mind. I didn't smoke. Instead, I left to go find Allie at Cameron's house. By the time I got there, they were already asleep. I went into the guest room and went to bed—still sober.

I never really understood why Mom and Dad thought Life360 was a good idea. It's not like they knew the area well enough to know where I was anyway. My friends and I hung out late at night all the time, and I tried to warn them about that. But still, I'd get a phone call from Mom every ten minutes asking where I was. It was driving me insane. The day they decided to get rid of the app, I swear I heard heaven's trumpets. I finally had my freedom back.

I shared a birthday with another girl in Pathway, so we had a joint party at one of the girls' houses. By then, I was finally starting to feel comfortable with transitioning out of outpatient, but of course, as soon as I started to feel settled, everything changed again. Now that I was eighteen, I got moved into the older group. It felt like every time I found some stability, they yanked it away. I hated it. Everyone else got to keep the same group of friends throughout the program, but mine was constantly shifting. It was exhausting.

My dad and I had a routine where he'd take me out for tacos on Thursdays when he came to the parent meetings during the summer. Every month or so, I'd go back to Cottonwood to see Sofi, my dad, and my cousins, staying for the weekend or just a day before heading back to Phoenix. Since he was stationed in New Mexico with the Air Force, I didn't see much of Jacob, and we still weren't talking much. Our relationship was just... nothing at that point. The only relationship that was really growing was the one with my mom. She kept coming to visit, and we'd spend time together—something nobody else seemed interested in doing. And honestly, I was still so resentful about everything that I didn't really care to make an effort with anyone else. If Sofi hadn't been at my dad's, I probably wouldn't have gone back at all.

Instead, I threw myself into my world in Phoenix—my friends at Pathway, and even the parents. I loved the parents, sometimes more than their kids. They were so nice to me, and I actually felt noticed when they talked to me. Cared for. A lot of them went out of their way to make sure I was okay, knowing I didn't have family close by. That meant something. It made me feel like I actually mattered to someone. I focused on that life and didn't think much about fixing things with anyone outside of it.

I loved being on my own in Phoenix, even when I found myself with nowhere to sleep at night. There were nights I slept in my car in what I hoped was a safe neighborhood. The older girls in the group would plan "girls' nights" and conveniently forget to invite me. They never accepted me, and since I had aged out of the younger group, I wasn't allowed to stay with my real friends anymore. That left me with one option—sleeping alone in my car. And still, even with that, I loved being there. Because no matter what, I was away from my family.

Even though I agreed to finish school, I hated it and didn't want to go. Most of the time, I just didn't. And even when I did, everything about how they did things there felt strange to me. Looking back, I don't think I was in the right place mentally to focus on school. There was still too much I needed to work through.

Chapter 9
Moving Home

As the holidays approached, a sense of stability settled over our lives. I had grown accustomed to Regan being in Arizona, our frequent phone calls, texts, and my Snapchat stalking becoming part of my routine. Though I missed her, I found comfort in knowing she was safe, focused, and continuing her journey. Tim and I had our own busy lives in Texas—weekends filled with friends, Houston Texans games, and other social events. For the first time in a long time, life didn't feel like it was hanging in the balance.

Regan had finally secured a job as a full-time nanny, caring for a young girl whose mother was raising her alone. She was earning her own money, which eased my constant worry about whether she had enough to eat or gas in her car to get where she needed to go. More importantly, she had a stable place to live, which further gave me peace of mind.

Meanwhile, I had completed my own journey through the Twelve Steps with my sponsor, a process that forced me to take a hard, honest look at myself. Examining my shortcomings, making amends to those I had hurt, and applying what I learned to my daily life had changed me. It was rare that I missed a Thursday night parent meeting—I had come to rely on them. But now, something had shifted. With Regan seven months sober, I wasn't just the desperate mother looking for hope. I had become someone who could extend that hope to others, offering reassurance to the parents just beginning their own heartbreaking journey.

Regan spent Thanksgiving in Cottonwood with her dad, Jacob, and Sofi, while Tim and I celebrated with the same friends we had spent the holiday with in years past. So much had changed since the last Thanksgiving—our lives had been turned upside down, but here we were, still standing. With these friends, there was no judgment, only love and acceptance, and I felt grateful to be in their presence.

Throughout the day, I exchanged texts and photos with both kids, small but meaningful reminders that, despite the distance, we were still connected. Then, that evening, my phone lit up with videos from Regan—she and Jacob, driving around, singing at the top of their lungs, being as silly and carefree as they had been when they were little. I could hear the laughter in their voices, see the lightheartedness in their expressions, and for a moment, it was as if all the pain, the years of tension and distance, were erased. I made a collage of their goofiness, a way to document this gift of nostalgia—so thankful to witness a glimpse of the love between them again.

Christmas came quickly on the heels of Thanksgiving, and I prepared our home the same way I always had—decorating the tree and the house with lights and ornaments and Christmas music playing nonstop. Regan wanted to come home for Christmas, but flights were expensive, and with her grandpa, aunt, and cousins from Iowa planning to visit after the New Year, we decided it made the most sense for her to come then. With just Tim and me at home, Christmas was notably quiet.

On Christmas Eve, we went to church and then attended a small gathering with a dear friend who had lost her husband earlier that year. Spending time with her brought comfort, breaking up some of the quiet stillness of the holiday for us. Christmas morning was simple—we unceremoniously opened gifts from our Iowa family, setting Regan's aside for when she arrived. The rest of the day passed peacefully, filled with football games, Christmas movies, and the kind of slow, easy moments that come when there's nothing pressing to do.

The family Regan was living with had their own Christmas traditions, and she planned to stay in her room while they celebrated—wanting to give them space for their family time. But they wouldn't hear of it. They insisted she join them, welcoming her into their festivities as if she were one of their own. To her surprise, she wasn't just a guest; she was included in their gift exchange, fully embraced as part of their family. Around lunchtime, my phone rang, and when I answered, all I could hear was Regan crying— happy tears. Through sniffles and laughter, she told me she had never felt so special and wanted as she did in that moment. My heart swelled with gratitude, overwhelmed by God's grace and the generosity of this family. It wasn't the Christmas we had planned, but it was exactly the Christmas she needed.

My dad, sister, niece, and nephew arrived the evening of January 3rd after a grueling fifteen-hour drive, weary but excited for the long-awaited reunion. The next evening, the three girls—my sister, niece, and I—drove to the airport to pick up Regan. My heart pounded as we neared the terminal, anticipation and nerves twisting together in my stomach. I couldn't wait to see her, but there was always that lingering fear—would she still be okay? Would this visit feel as joyful as we hoped?

We stopped at a gas station to use the restroom after leaving the airport, and the moment we got out of the car, her cousin—just eighteen months younger—embraced her right there in the parking lot. Their hug was sweet and unbreakable, like two lost souls finally finding each other again. My sister and I exchanged tearful glances, overwhelmed by the depth of their connection. They had never lived in the same state and never had the luxury of growing up side by side, yet the love between them had never wavered. Watching them hold onto each other so tightly, I knew in my heart that Regan was truly cherished.

Once again, I felt an immense wave of gratitude for the warmth and acceptance that surrounded her. The fear of judgment had never fully left me—I braced myself for words or actions that could wound her, set her back, and make her question her worth. I wanted to shield her from anything that might push her toward relapse, but I was beginning to realize that my own anxiety, my need to control every detail, wasn't the answer. Her choices still affected me deeply, but I was learning that the real work—the hardest work—was mine to do.

After everyone greeted her with warm hugs and snapped pictures in front of the Christmas tree together, we settled in to watch her open her presents. Laughter and easy conversation filled the room as she caught everyone up on how she was doing, and I couldn't help but marvel at how different she looked—how different she *felt*. Her blonde hair had grown since my last visit, now just shy of grazing her shoulders. She sat on the couch nearest the Christmas tree, her face lit with excitement, dressed in a navy sweater dress paired with over-the-knee boots and a chambray button-up worn cardigan-style. Casual, chic, and effortlessly feminine—so different from the drab, oversized clothes she had hidden beneath the year before. A year ago, she had looked lost, swallowed by her own sadness, her baggy layers a shield from the world. But now? She was starting to *glow* again.

The following day, we welcomed friends into our home—people who had watched Regan grow up and were just as eager as we were to wrap their arms around her. One by one, they embraced her, showering her with love and admiration, snapping more pictures in front of the Christmas tree as if to capture the moment forever.

The Texans game played in the background, but for once, I couldn't have cared less about the score. At halftime, someone grabbed a bag of oversized cotton snowballs, and in an instant, the living room erupted into laughter as we hurled them at one another like carefree kids. The air was filled with joy, and for the first time in a long time, it felt *light*—no tension, no worry, just the pure happiness of having my daughter back where she belonged. I looked around, taking it all in. The love. The laughter. The *normalcy.* And I realized that no present under the tree could have ever compared to this. Regan was home. That was the only Christmas gift I needed.

Her grandpa, aunt, and cousins drove back to Iowa the following morning, and she stayed only another day or so. The plan was for her to be at Pathway for an indefinite future, but the visit did feel like a turning point. Something shifted having her home, but I didn't pay much attention to it, thinking it was more likely my own wishful thinking than reality. Her staying in Arizona or going anywhere else, including home, was not my decision to make. But just two weeks later, I received a Snapchat message from her. She was smiling, eyes closed, head tilted up, the dark sky littered with stars, and the message across her chin read:

```
I miss you a lot. I've been think-
ing a lot 'cause I kinda wanna
come home
```

It was 11:11 p.m.

I called her immediately, needing to hear the words for myself—to know if she truly meant what I thought she did. She did.

For the past couple of weeks, we had been deep in the process of securing a small apartment for her and Sofi, finalizing the lease, and preparing for what we thought would be her next step. But now, she was having second thoughts. She told me that after ten months in Arizona, she felt ready to move on with her life. The trip home had stirred something in her, pulling at her heartstrings and making her homesick in a way she hadn't expected.

As much as my heart leaped at her words, I kept my emotions in check. "Sleep on it," I told her gently. "If you still feel the same tomorrow, we'll figure everything out."

She didn't change her mind, and things moved quite rapidly. She talked to Boomer first to tell him what she wanted to do and get his blessing. He wasn't fully supportive of her, but he also couldn't make her stay. It was a two-and-a-half-year program for a reason, and she'd not even completed a year yet. However, he also acknowledged that she didn't have her family nearby as all the other kids did, so it was natural for her to want to go back home at some point. Ultimately, she was sure this was what she wanted, and he wished her well. I purchased a flight to Tucson for the following Saturday morning, with the plan of her picking me up and driving us and Sofi in her car back to Texas. It was about a twenty-hour drive.

She didn't get more than an hour or two of sleep the night before she was to leave Phoenix, as she and her friends wanted to spend as much time together as possible. She was emotional leaving those she'd really grown close to, as well as the family who had so graciously accepted her as one of their own. I had a 6 a.m. flight, which meant a very short night for me as well, and probably not the best plan for a very long drive. But the excitement of this change was the driving force making it happen.

It was about 9:30 in the morning when Regan picked me up in Tucson, and we headed east. She'd packed all her things in a couple of plastic totes and bags, folded up the back seats in her Honda Element, and had it all thoughtfully placed in the entire back of the vehicle so it was flat on top. She put several blankets over the surface, making what looked like a bed, and had pillows and stuffed animals decorating it. This is where Sofi would lie and ride for the trip. And where one of us at a time could lie down and nap if we needed to. It was truly genius and worked out perfectly.

The trip started off strong—our voices filling the car as we talked nonstop, catching up on everything and nothing all at once. Laughter came easily, the kind that made our sides ache and our eyes water. Sofi settled onto the blankets in the back as if she realized this was going to be a longer car ride than normal. The miles stretched behind us effortlessly.

Since Jacob was stationed at Holloman Air Force Base—only about an hour off our route—we made plans to stop and have dinner with him. By the time we pulled into the Chili's parking lot in Alamogordo, the sun was dipping below the horizon, washing the desert in hues of pink and orange. Seeing her brother was both familiar and strange. Their banter picked up where it had left off, but there was an unspoken acknowledgment of time lost, of separate lives being lived. Still, dinner was warm and easy, a brief moment of normalcy before we hit the road again.

Night had fully settled in by the time we left. The darkness outside made the car feel smaller and cozier. Regan drove for hours, determination written across her face as she kept her hands steady on the wheel. I stayed awake beside her, fighting my own exhaustion, unwilling to risk her drifting off. Sometime after midnight, she exhaled deeply, rubbing her eyes. "I need to rest for a bit," she admitted.

We pulled into a gas station, where she climbed into the bed in the back with Sofi, asleep almost instantly. I slid into the driver's seat and pushed forward, but my exhaustion was relentless. Every mile blurred into the next, my eyes growing heavier despite my efforts. After five hours, unable to fight it any longer, I spotted a church parking lot and pulled in. I only meant to rest for a quick nap, but the next thing I knew, Regan was awake. She sat up, confused, peering out the window in the dawn of the new morning at the empty lot before turning to me. "Why didn't you wake me up?" she asked, obviously annoyed.

I mumbled something about being too tired, but she was already swinging into action. "We're so close—I want to be home already." Playfully and seriously, she kicked me out of the driver's seat and took over. Within two hours, the familiar sight of our neighborhood greeted us. We didn't bother unpacking right away. Instead, we walked inside, kicked off our shoes, and collapsed onto our beds. Home at last.

Instead of moving back into her old room, Regan decided that the environment had too many bad memories attached to it. She had used drugs in her room and was in a very dark place when she last spent time there. So, she set up her room in our upstairs game room, which she turned into a small kitchenless apartment. She had a bedroom area, a living area, her own bathroom with a shower, a vanity nook, and a big air hockey table that she put everything else on top of like a catch-all. The walls were decorated with photos and letters from her friends from her time at Pathway, and Sofi and Charlie became friends quickly.

She settled in over a few days while Tim and I went back to work and our normal schedules. It didn't take long at all to realize that she had little to do here since all of her friends were in Arizona, and she hadn't been in touch with anyone here in over a year. She also didn't have a job and wasn't in school, so we talked to her about both of these things. Her reaction was positive, and she was open to looking for a job, but she was also cautious about what kind of job she would accept. She'd worked in restaurants prior to her going to Arizona and knew that drug use was prevalent there, so this was not an option for her. We made some suggestions for places she could look into and expected her to spend her time doing so. Only it didn't feel like she was, even when she said she was. Days passed, and she would be gone in the afternoons and evenings, saying she was job hunting and then spending time with old girlfriends from high school. One friend in particular made me uneasy, knowing they had previously used together. Regan assured me she was no longer using, and it was a safe relationship for her. Maybe that was true. Not everyone who uses drugs in high school ends up needing treatment. I wanted to believe her, so I let myself do just that.

About every few days, it seemed, Regan would tell me one of her friends at Pathway had relapsed. There were upwards of at least nine over a very short amount of time, including two of her closest friends. This pattern was distressing for both of us, but in different ways. For me, it made relapse far too real of a possibility, and I knew the fear that a parent feels when their child makes the choice to gamble with his/her life in this way. It got to the point where every time she talked to someone from the group, there was another person who had relapsed. Regan would express frustration at why this was happening, but also that the responsibility was on them. She cared about them, but also had to protect her own recovery, so she limited her interactions with many of them.

After a couple of weeks with no real progress in finding a job, we started to get impatient. It was still nice having her around, but she couldn't just exist like this long term. She was sober, which was great, but she'd moved home to move forward. I refused to give her money and only did so to fill her car with gas when she said she was job hunting. We discussed options for finishing high school, but she resisted the idea. I researched some online options, but there were a lot of hoops to jump through, and she dragged her feet on making a decision about it at all. One thing she was one hundred percent adamant about was that she would not be going back to high school in person. This was out of the question. I was willing to accommodate that if we could find a viable option. We really weren't excited about her just getting a GED, as everyone we talked to told us that a high school diploma was better for getting into college. It was far too soon to discuss college, and I wasn't sure if she'd ever want to pursue it, but I wanted to make sure she had the opportunity if she chose to in the future.

I was getting ready for bed when my phone buzzed at 10:13 p.m.

Regan: Are you still up?
Me: Yes. Why?
Regan: Because I wanted to talk to you before you go to bed.
Me: Ok. How far away are you?
Regan: About 15 minutes...

She had only been home a few weeks, and while things seemed fine on the surface, I still carried a lingering sense of unease. But there was no urgency in her message, no panic—just a simple request. I was curious what she wanted to talk about.

I heard her come in just after 10:30. Her footsteps were quick up the stairs. She didn't hesitate, but I did. I waited a minute or two before I went up after her. Tim was already asleep.

When I walked into her room, she was sitting cross-legged on the couch, just waiting for me to sit down next to her. Sofi lay curled up beside her. She looked… normal—not nervous, not upset. I asked casually, "What's up?"

She took a deep breath, exhaling slowly before speaking. "I relapsed." The words landed like a punch to my gut, knocking the air from my lungs. My mind scrambled to make sense of it. *No. She's been sober for almost a year. She wouldn't throw that away.* I searched her face. She wasn't high—at least not right now. She wasn't defensive, either. Just calm.

"When?" I finally managed.

"A few days ago."

I blinked. My mouth opened, then closed. I wanted to rewind, to pretend I hadn't heard her, but the words were already there, hanging in the air between us.

"But… you were almost a year sober." My voice cracked. "Regan, why?"

She hesitated, looking down at her hands. "I don't know." Then she looked back at me, voice steady. "I just don't know if I want to be sober."

The room felt like it was shrinking around me. "So what now?" I asked, my voice hollow.

She swallowed hard. "I know your rule about not using in

your house. I respect that." A pause. "So... I'm moving out until I figure out what I want to do."

I stared at her. *Did she really just say that?*

"Tonight."

My breath hitched. It was surreal, like watching a movie of someone else's life. Not mine. Not hers. I wanted to say something—*fight for her, convince her, beg her to stay.* But what could I say? She had already made her choice.

The silence stretched. Finally, I nodded. "Okay." My voice barely made a sound.

We both stood up, and she wrapped her arms around me. "I love you, Mom."

I clung to her, wishing I didn't have to let go. "I love you, too."

When I pulled away, I cleared my throat and forced out the only other words I could manage. "Take Sofi with you. She's your responsibility."

I walked downstairs in a daze, my legs moving on autopilot.

My mind was still spinning as I crawled into bed. Upstairs, I could hear her moving around, quietly packing her things. Every rustle, every zip of a bag felt like another piece of her slipping away. About half an hour later, she left without a word. The house felt impossibly quiet. Empty all over again.

Tears spilled down my cheeks as I whispered to Tim what had happened. He struggled to understand, shaking his head. "It's her choice," he said finally. "She has to figure it out." I knew he was angry—not at her, but at how this was breaking me all over again.

Sleep never came. But when morning came, I got up, got dressed, and went to work—pretending everything was normal.

Thankfully, I had moms from Pathway that I could reach out

to for support, and I did. Telling my friends that she'd relapsed and left again and that I didn't know where she was was so incredibly hard. Few understood, and others asked me why I let her go. She was eighteen, all of one hundred and five pounds, no money, no job, with a car and a dog. My answer was always that she is an adult, and it wasn't my job to stop her or chase after her. Did that make me sound like a monster? Do good moms chase after their kids when they leave to go get high? What happens when you find them? I had my boundary of no using in my home, and I wasn't budging on that. The only reasonable thing to do was to let her go and figure it out for herself. The next question was, "But what if something bad happens to her, or what if she dies?" My answer to that was that I knew God had her, and I had to let Him be in control. I was not capable of controlling the situation or my daughter, and I wanted *her* to make the choice to be sober. This was not going to be easy.

I'm not going to tell you that I handled this situation well. I was miserable, and I cried often. I forced myself to go to work every day and put on a happy face. Those who knew me could tell it was fake, but nobody held it against me. The worst part was just not knowing who she was with, what was happening to her, or where she was. But in many ways, it was easier not to know. As the days passed, going through my regular routine did get less painful, but I knew from my parent support groups, the Twelve Steps, my sponsor, and all the books I'd read about addiction that what I was doing (or not doing) was the right thing. **LET HER GO.** I'd done it before, and I could do it again. But this wasn't just letting go—it was being dragged, kicking, and screaming back into the fire I thought I had escaped. The smoke was thick, choking out my hope, the heat blistering as I braced myself for the agony of losing her all over again.

We didn't have much contact during the time she was in her relapse. I reached out to her only two or three times to tell her I loved her and missed her and hoped she was doing well. Her responses usually came hours later or the next day with what seemed like an old picture of her looking good and a cheerful "I love you, too." No details, nothing else, but then again, I hadn't asked. I wasn't sure I wanted to know, anyway. One afternoon, driving home from work, I saw her car driving on Main Street in Tomball (a town near Magnolia). She was a few cars ahead of me, and since she drove a Honda Element, she was easy to spot. It is a unique car and we called it lovingly "The Toaster" (it looked like a blue toaster). Anyway, it was definitely her. My heart jumped out of my chest when I saw her car. *She's alive, at least, I thought.* It took every ounce of my being not to follow her. She went straight, and I made my right turn onto Cherry Street as I did every day. I didn't know how to feel about seeing her car and almost seeing her. There wasn't much to be happy about, but I guess I felt a twinge of hope that she was okay and still had her car.

Each day felt like a year. It was as if time had slowed down to almost a standstill. I knew I needed support, but the online parent meetings didn't seem like enough. I wanted face-to-face support—people with whom I could be in the same room to try to work through this. The Al-Anon meeting I had gone to that one time was still on Tuesdays at 7 p.m. I went back two days after she left and every Tuesday after that. The first one was awkward because I didn't know anyone, and there were quite a few attendees. But because I'd been attending parent meetings for the better part of the past year, I was comfortable enough to share that my eighteen-year-old daughter had relapsed after almost eleven months of sobriety. They loved and supported me while tears fell down my cheeks, offering me hope and community. I listened to each one of them share their experiences and heartbreaks as well. I never went to one meeting where I didn't feel better after leaving. It didn't take long to become familiar with everyone in the room and to be able to offer support and encouragement in the same way I received from each of them. One man I didn't know gave me a handwritten message after a meeting where I'd shared a portion of my story of my daughter's drug use. It said, "You are an example that a mother's love is given without reservation or limits."

I dug into my *Parent to Parent* book to find wisdom and guidance during this time as well. Leaning into the Twelve Steps and the experiences of those who have gone before me was something I needed to do. I'll share a couple of passages that helped me keep moving forward and eventually find peace and even joy in my days. First is from the book *Parent to Parent:*

> Today's Reminder: Despite what I think should be happening, I will remember that God has a better idea. Everything is working out perfectly. AA has an actual bumper sticker that reads, 'Expect a Miracle.' It doesn't tell us that we deserve a miracle; it says we can expect one. There is a difference. Expecting a miracle means that we expect something wonderful is going to happen—we aren't putting a specific expectation on some 'thing.' We are not expecting it not to rain tomorrow. We are expecting a good day,

no matter the weather.[1]

This quote was found online by a friend, who is not in recovery, who thought of me. Although the author is unknown, I printed it out and taped it on my bathroom mirror, where it remained for more than five years. It is also on the wall in my office:

> One of the hardest lessons I've
> learned is that I can't always
> keep those I love from jumping
> off a cliff, figuratively speaking.
> Nor should I in some cases. Some-
> times, I may be preventing God
> from doing His work in them. Un-
> like us, God often allows those
> He loves to suffer the consequenc-
> es for bad decisions. When we re-
> fuse to ever do the same, we may
> be preventing valuable lessons
> learned and therefore long-term
> growth. So we can't always pre-
> vent others from jumping, but we
> can always be ready to catch them
> when they fall (Luke 15:11-32).

Twenty-three days after Regan left our home, not knowing if she wanted to be sober, she called me. It was a Friday, and I had just gotten to work. I'd walked to the back of the office to get my laptop out of the safe in the closet when my phone rang. I heard it but didn't make it back to my desk in time to answer it. When I saw that I'd missed a call from Regan, I was again shocked but

---

1 Furtney, S. *Parent to Parent: Experience, Strength, and Hope Shared by Parents of Young Drug Addicts and Alcoholics*. Meek Publishing, 2012.

also desperate to know why she had called. Was she okay? Did she get hurt? Did she change her mind? I pushed the questions away, quickly called her back, and waited for her to answer. After only a couple of rings, she picked up, "Mom!" I apologized for missing her call. She said she thought I didn't want to talk to her when I hadn't answered. Seriously?

"How are you?" I asked.

"I hate this life, and I want to be sober. I've called a couple of places for help, and I left a message for Boomer. I'll…" I cut her off.

"Come home!"

"Are you sure?"

"Yes. We will figure this out. Where are you?" She was about an hour away from home, and she had Sofi and a friend with her who, after listening to her talk to me and her other sober friends from Pathway on that drive home, decided he, too, wanted to try the sober life. She vowed to help him.

We talked for only a few minutes, as she had more phone calls she wanted to make. She sounded happy, and I believed that she was done. She was not allowed to be at the house alone, as we had changed the locks after she left. She had to wait until Tim got home, which was mid-afternoon. I told her she would need to talk to him and ask him if it was okay for her to move back home, and that we could discuss it more when I got there. I called Tim to tell him the news and let him know she'd be coming to talk to him before I got home. We welcomed her back with open arms, and she let us know that she didn't expect us to, that she was not expecting to be able to come back home after what she'd done.

Regan offered to go back to Pathway to do treatment over again; whatever she had to do, she would do it. I put the brakes on, appreciating her willingness to do all of that, but I needed to process this through in a more careful, thought-out way. She'd spent ten months in a solid recovery program, learning all about the Twelve Steps, sticking with winners, utilizing support groups, and more. What she didn't do was apply that knowledge once she left the "bubble" of Pathway. She hadn't gone to one meeting since moving home, or done anything other than keep in touch with her friends there. It would take more than that to stay sober. What if we found a support system here, like she had in Arizona, and she applied her recovery knowledge to her life going forward? After some discussion, we decided that we would start with this, and if things didn't go well, she would go back to Pathway. It was helpful having a backup plan, but I was hopeful she could make it work being sober here.

One might ask why we didn't think to find recovery support in Texas prior to or right after she moved back home. It's a good question, and my answer to that would be that I honestly didn't put much thought into it at the time. She still had her sober friends at Pathway, and I was still attending the parent meetings every week, so it seemed like we were still involved. I know that I did talk with Regan about finding an AA meeting here that she could go to, and she said she intended to do that, but I didn't push it. Again, it wasn't my job to structure a recovery program for her or even determine what that looked like. That was for her to figure out and implement. However, I could have made attending meetings regularly a condition for her moving home, and I probably should have. I think there was a part of me that believed that she was "fixed," that she really hadn't had a drug addiction, and that maybe meetings weren't necessary for her to stay sober. Obviously, the part about her being cured of wanting to use drugs was erroneous, but what her relapse taught me was invaluable.

I learned that she does have a drug addiction or substance use disorder and that she will need to maintain sobriety for the rest of her life. This is a very hard pill to swallow for a middle-aged man or woman, but it is exceptionally difficult for a young adult or an eighteen-year-old. This fact brings another lesson: working a recovery program and/or continuing to grow and heal is a requirement for living and maintaining a productive, sober life.

I also learned that there can be value in relapsing. While I would never hope for it or wish it on anyone, it did teach me that detachment is a powerful tool for not only letting my loved one learn how to make choices and reap the consequences of those choices but also for my own peace and healing. I am never in control of another person's actions, so it is best if I focus my energy on finding peace regardless of others' actions. Letting my daughter go and figure out what she wanted for herself was the right decision, even though it was gut-wrenchingly hard to stick to. Detachment in love and relying on God's faithfulness is my path forward when things seem headed for disaster.

REGAN

I drove to my dad's for Thanksgiving, and Jacob was there on leave. Hanging out with him that day and evening felt like how we used to be when we were kids—for the first time in a really long time. For a moment, it gave me hope that maybe we could have a real relationship again. But after we both left and went back to our own lives, he stayed distant, just like before. It was like nothing had ever changed.

For Christmas, I honestly don't even know if my dad or my aunt and uncle ever really called to invite me. They lived the closest, but they never put much effort into being involved in my life, and I was done trying, too. So, I didn't offer to drive out there.

Instead, I planned to stay at Ella's, figuring I'd just hang out upstairs in my room while her family did their Christmas traditions. I didn't want to be in the way.

Everyone had gone downstairs, but then I heard them calling my name. I hesitated, but they kept calling for me to come down. When I finally did, they included me in everything—like really included me. They even got me presents. It was so sweet, and I had so much fun with them. After opening everything, I stood up and gave Mama Maureen a big hug, and out of nowhere, I just started crying happy tears. Then the whole family joined in, and suddenly, we were in this big, cheesy group hug, and every single person was crying. I was not expecting them to love me like that. It was overwhelming, in the best way. It was the first time I'd ever been a part of a family that felt so whole—one that actually loved each other and loved me, too.

I stayed in Phoenix through New Year's because Pathway had a big lock-in function with all the kids and parents, and there was no way I was going to miss that. I planned my trip back to Texas for right after the new year. I did feel homesick sometimes, and it had been a while since I'd been back, so I was actually looking forward to the trip. My grandpa, aunt, and cousins all came to Texas from Iowa at the same time, which made it even better. I loved getting to chat with everyone, but my favorite part of the trip was hanging out with my cousin, Taya. She was closest to me in age, and I'd always loved spending time with her, but we never got to hang out as much as I wished we had growing up.

It was a really nice visit, but short, and by the end of it, I was excited to get back to my friends in Arizona.

I had already been thinking about moving back home before my trip to Texas, but spending time there really sealed the deal.

I was starting to feel complacent in the group—doing the same things over and over again. I was ready to grow up and have a real life. Pathway wasn't my forever place, and I didn't want to end up like some of the young adults there, still living like teenagers in their twenties. Being in the older group gave me a whole new perspective, and I knew I was ready for the next step.

Leaving was harder than I thought it would be. Saying goodbye to the people I loved was awful. But it was more complicated than that. Not everyone was supportive when I told people I was moving back home. To my surprise, some of them were actually really rude about it—telling me I was making a terrible decision and that I was definitely going to relapse. The more I heard that, the more determined I was to do it and prove them wrong. I couldn't understand why they were being so mean about it, especially since I was the only kid in the program with no family there and no one outside of the group. It hurt my feelings, but at the same time, it made me feel even more confident that I was making the right choice. Why would I want to stay around people who weren't supportive of me moving forward with my life?

My real friends—the ones who actually cared about me—responded with love. They encouraged me and told me we would always be friends no matter what. Saying goodbye to them was the hardest part. I didn't want to sleep on my last night because I wanted to soak up every minute I had left with them before leaving to pick up my mom at the airport the next morning.

I was exhausted, but I made it to the Tucson airport, grabbed Mom, and we headed on our way. I drove almost the entire trip back to Texas. We made a detour to see Jacob, which was a little weird since our relationship was still rocky, and we didn't talk much in daily life. But I loved him, and it was good to see him and meet his girlfriend, who was really nice.

About fifteen hours into the drive, I finally hit a wall and let Mom take over. Only when I woke up did I find her asleep in the front seat. How is it that I drove all that way on barely any sleep, and she couldn't even manage a few hours to get us home? I was so annoyed. I immediately kicked her out of the driver's seat and finished the trip myself. We pulled into the driveway just a couple of hours later. Annoying as that was, the drive itself was actually fun and a trip I'll never forget.

As excited as I was to finally be home, I don't think I had really connected the dots between being home and leaving Pathway. I knew I was moving states away, but somehow, I still assumed everything was going to be exactly like it was in Phoenix—just with the only difference being that I lived at home. But really quickly, I started missing my friends, and not having anyone to hang out with anymore was way harder than I expected. I didn't want to reconnect with anyone from my old life, but then I started hearing that person after person at Pathway was relapsing. One friend after another was struggling, and it made me start second-guessing my own sobriety. I had nobody locally I could turn to for support, and now, a lot of my friends in Arizona were using again and couldn't be there for me either.

One night, a friend from Arizona, whom I'd heard had relapsed, reached out to me. We had chatted off and on throughout the night, but the last time we talked, he wasn't making any sense. He was slurring his words, mumbling, and I could tell something was really off. I didn't know where he was, but at some point, he told me he had shot up heroin while we were on the phone. As we kept talking, he started nodding off. Immediately, I panicked. Was he overdosing? Was he okay? I had no idea what to do or who to call. I just stayed on the phone, calling his name over and over, trying to get him to talk to me. But all I heard was silence. He wasn't responding. Eventually, I hung up, but that whole experience was terrifying. I had no way of knowing if he was okay, and it left me feeling so shaken up.

Everything just started piling up. I felt alone. I felt desperate to have my old life back—the one where all my friends were still sober and I had people to lean on. I felt my happiness slipping away, along with my motivation to get a job or finish school. I didn't know how to cope, and the truth was, I had never really accepted Step One—that my life had been unmanageable *because* of drugs. To me, it wasn't the drugs that made my life unmanageable—it was people. It was my family. It was all the people who had hurt me and lied to me for years.

I convinced myself that I just needed something to help me sleep, so I bought a dab pen, a vape for smoking THC wax (an extremely concentrated form of THC), thinking I would only use it once a day. That lasted three days before I was using it constantly. From there, it spiraled fast. I got back in contact with my old friends and started using with them again. After about a week, I knew I needed to tell my mom.

That night, I sat upstairs in my room and just told her directly, "I've been using, and I don't know if I want to be sober. I don't know what I want right now, but I have to talk to you about it because I do love you to death, and I know your rules. I'm not going to disrespect you, so I'm going to pack my stuff and leave."

She didn't say much. What could she really say? But she did tell me to take Sofi with me because she was my responsibility. I didn't argue. She was right.

I threw my stuff in my car, grabbed Sofi, and went to get high with my friends. I crashed at an apartment with a couple of girls for a few nights, but my using got worse—more and more, both in how much and how often. Eventually, I ended up in some run-down house in a college town about an hour away, surrounded by people I barely knew.

At first, I kept telling myself that this was fun, that I was free, and that I could do whatever I wanted. But the drugs weren't working the way they used to. The numbness that once brought peace and happiness was gone. Instead, it numbed the good parts of me and made everything bad so much worse. My mind wouldn't shut off anymore. Getting high only made me cry and throw up blood. I'd pass out, wake up, and do it all over again.

During that time, I started calling my friend Matt from Pathway. He was the only person I could think of who still cared about me. I called him a lot, crying, desperate for love and support, but I was always high. Finally, one day, he told me, "I love you, and I don't want you to die. But I can't do this anymore. I'll always be here for you, but not while you're actively trying to kill yourself. I can't watch you do this." Then he told me he wasn't going to talk to me again unless I was sober. And he hung up.

I just sat there, staring at my phone, devastated.

After that, I felt like I had lost everything. Everyone who had ever loved me was gone. I started thinking about my life and whether I could get sober again. I even looked up treatment centers near me just to see what was out there. But it took a couple more days of using, feeling miserable, before I woke up on March 15th and thought, "I don't want to do this anymore."

I kept searching for treatment options, but eventually, I just picked up the phone and called my mom.

She didn't answer.

My stomach dropped. I figured she was done with me, that she had finally given up after everything I'd put her through. But then, just a minute or two later, my phone rang. It was her. I answered right away.

The second she picked up, I blurted out, "I don't want to do this anymore. I don't want to use drugs. I found some places I could go, but I just—I just want to be sober."

She cut me off. "Come home."

I was so shocked. I asked, "Really?"

I had already been preparing myself to figure this out on my own. I had no money and no real place to go, but I was going to figure it out somehow. I had zero expectation of being allowed back home. But the second she said it, I felt this wave of relief. I was going home.

Talking to Tim was hard. He wasn't exactly thrilled with me after everything I'd done, and I couldn't blame him. He wanted to know what was different this time. Why should he believe me now?

I told him the truth—I didn't want to die anymore. When I first started using drugs, I didn't care if I lived or not. Honestly, I preferred not to. But I had come so close to death, more times than I wanted to admit, and I realized I wanted more for myself. I didn't just want to get sober to make everyone happy—I wanted it for me. I told him I was done with drugs and that I never wanted to go near them again. For me, drugs equaled death. I knew that if I ever relapsed again, that's what would happen. I couldn't use manageably. I couldn't pretend I had any kind of control. And the scary part? I no longer had any desire to even try.

But the thing that hit me the hardest, the thing that really made me see how bad it had gotten, was Sofi.

Sofi had been the one thing that kept me alive through everything. When I had nothing and no one, I had her. I knew she needed me, and that was the only reason I could never actually go through with killing myself. I never would have wanted to hurt her by abandoning her.

But when I was high, when my using got out of control, I forgot she even existed. I don't remember having her with me at all during those weeks. I didn't feed her. I didn't take care of her. I have no idea where she was or how she survived. How could I love this dog more than anything in the world and not think twice about her when I was using?

Even now, I feel absolutely horrible about it. It's something I don't know if I'll ever forgive myself for. But it also showed me, in the most brutal way possible, that I was not in control. Drugs had a grip on me that I could never afford to risk again. I was an addict. And I was finally ready to admit it.

Chapter 10
Sobriety

The first thing we did after Regan came back home was to take her car to get new tires. She'd driven home from over an hour away on a donut, and her low tire light was on. I asked how she had gotten a flat tire, but she only offered a vague response, which probably meant she didn't really know because she was high at the time. Instead of addressing that, I just told her we'd get her car back to being safe for her to drive again. We had such a good time that day, she was happy, and we interacted with ease. She looked beautiful, and I snapped some pictures of her driving to capture the moment. Somehow, the conversation turned to religion due to a comment I must have made about God or church or something religious. When she snapped at me, "I'm NOT a Christian!" it surprised me. I felt an instantaneous stab to my heart, but tried not to skip a beat, knowing this was not an argument I would win. She would need to come around to her faith on her own, in her own time. My response was simply, "Okay." And we changed the subject. My heart knew she would come around, but she was clearly still angry at God for all the things she'd endured during her short life. Rome wasn't built in a day. This was a marathon, not a sprint. *Okay, God, help me lead her to You.*

As happy as I was to have Regan back home and sober again, it became imperative to get to work finding support. After she relapsed and went back out using, it occurred to me that I wasn't ever going to be enough for her to stay sober, nor did I want that responsibility. Her recovery could not solely rest on my support of her, though I would always be supportive of her sobriety. Fortunately, I didn't have to tell Regan this. She was proactive in finding AA meetings to go to, and started attending one she particularly liked on a regular basis. She loved AA but wasn't a big fan of there only being older people in the meetings. At eighteen, it was very hard to relate to adults as they were in a different phase of life than hers. There were a few women in her meetings who were intentional in reaching out to her and mentoring her. She pretty quickly found a sponsor she liked a lot, but it would not last long due to the woman moving away.

A couple of weeks after I started attending Al-Anon during Regan's relapse, I walked into a meeting and immediately recognized another mom—Mary—whose daughter had gone to both school and church with Regan. I froze for a moment, as did she. Seeing a familiar face in a support group shouldn't have been such a surprise, yet we were both visibly stunned. The unspoken question hung between us: *What are you doing here?*

Leave it to God to orchestrate this moment—placing us in the same room, knowing we were already friends, that our daughters had once been close, and that we needed each other now more than ever. As we talked, we learned that both of our daughters had battled addiction, completed treatment, and were now in recovery. It was a bittersweet revelation—one that neither of us would have chosen, but that instantly bonded us in a way only another parent in this journey could understand. Reconnecting with Mary was an unexpected gift, despite the less-than-ideal circumstances.

I continued attending Al-Anon for a few more months while also rejoining the Thursday night parent meetings at Pathway online. By now, Pathway had introduced a video feature for parents who couldn't attend in person, allowing me not just to listen but to see and be seen. It made the experience feel more personal, more connected—like I was still part of the community that had supported me through the hardest days. Those meetings continued to be a lifeline, a steady presence in my life for the next few years.

In April, I came upon an article in a local newspaper about suicide, its causes, statistics, and treatment, which caught my attention. The agency interviewed for the story was Mosaics of Mercy, whose mission is to connect people with mental health needs to providers and resources. Even though Regan was going to an AA group and I was attending my support groups, she was frequently commenting that she wished to find more sober people her own age. I called Mosaics of Mercy to see if they could help us. A wonderful woman took my call, listened to our needs, and discussed a few options that we could explore. Regan chose one to check out. It was a newly opened non-profit recovery center in a town about thirty minutes north of us. The owner was a chemical dependency counselor, and her mission was to provide support and fun sober activities and events to her clients. This seemed like a step in the right direction. We scheduled a meeting with Kerry, the owner, the following week.

Meeting with Kerry, along with Regan, was a learning experience for me. What I thought was the problem that needed to be solved was not completely the same as my daughter's assessment. In that meeting, I learned that she suffers from anxiety. How did I not know that? They discussed some options for addressing her mental health and her goals for moving forward in the next year. I thought we were there to help her utilize her recovery tools to stay sober, but this was much broader than that. Despite all the books I'd read, meetings I'd attended, and experiences I'd had in the recovery community, there were still things that I just didn't grasp until they smacked me in the face. My daughter has mental health issues and struggles with self-esteem. Of course, she does. How could she have gotten here if she didn't? Being sober doesn't cure that. It just paves the way for the real work to be done.

Kerry scheduled an appointment for Regan to return on her own and meet with a recovery coach, someone who could help her set goals and take concrete steps toward achieving them. One of the first and most pressing goals was finishing high school. She wasn't making any progress in finding a job, and we knew that her chances of securing one were slim without a diploma.

At this stage, her options for completing high school were limited due to her age and how long she'd been out. Earning her GED was the most viable path forward, but I dreaded bringing it up. I knew she would resist. School had always been a source of frustration and struggle for her, made worse by an undiagnosed processing issue that distorted the way she saw words on a page. By the time it was discovered at the start of her senior year, she had already turned to drugs to cope. Years of struggling with reading and comprehension had chipped away at her confidence, leaving her feeling stupid and incapable of success. It was no wonder she avoided school in Arizona—deep down, she didn't believe she was capable of finishing.

I brought up the idea of getting her GED one night in May, hopeful that I'd found a solution she could accept. There was a review course at the local community college—a six-week program designed to refresh her on the material and prepare her for each of the four subject tests. The cost was minimal, and I was more than willing to cover it if she agreed to go. But the second I started explaining it to her, I saw the resistance in her face.

Her arms folded. Her shoulders tensed. I kept talking, trying to make it sound like a good opportunity, but she wasn't buying it. And when I finally told her it was really her only option, her resistance turned to anger.

"No. I'm not doing that," she snapped.

The conversation spiraled into an argument. She hated being backed into a corner, and I hated having to push her, but this wasn't optional. Finishing high school—one way or another—was necessary for her to have a future, find a decent job, and build a life beyond this chapter. She fought me, but I didn't back down. Finally, after a tense standoff, she muttered an irritated, "Fine." I gave her the information she needed to register for the course.

Then she turned to go upstairs, and the weight of what had just happened hit me all at once. My chest tightened so hard it felt like I was suffocating. *What have I done?* My heart pounded as the worst thought imaginable gripped me. *What if I pushed too hard? What if I just caused her to relapse?* I stood there frozen, my mind spiraling in a hundred directions. Every fear I'd worked so hard to keep at bay came rushing in—was I walking her straight back into her old life? Should I have just let her figure things out on her own? *What if one argument with me was all it took to undo everything?* The fear was overwhelming, and I'm not sure how long it took me to start breathing again.

Despite her reluctance, Regan went to the local community college campus, jumped through several hoops to get herself registered for the GED review course, and then was told the only one available to her at that time was about an hour away. They met each weekday evening for a couple of hours for six weeks. She came home unhappy about this, but surprisingly determined to just get it over with. We purchased the required workbook, and she started pretty much immediately. I know she didn't love it, but she did attend every class and said that the review was much needed. After a few weeks, she decided to go ahead and take the first of the subject tests, which she passed. A couple of days later, she passed another. Then she paused, and I could see the fear seeping in.

Whether this was the right thing to do or not, I did it anyway. I offered to buy her a plane ticket to Arizona to visit her Pathway friends if she passed the final two tests and got her GED. She had wanted to go back really badly in June for an event, and time was growing short. This did motivate her, and she took and passed both of the remaining tests on the same day. We rejoiced!

I got online and purchased her flight, which was just a few days away. I'm not sure I'd advocate for bribery, but this was a milestone that was a struggle to reach, and I was willing to do almost anything in my power to see her succeed. Not only did she finally finish high school, but with this accomplishment came a boost of confidence and self-esteem that she needed even more than the GED. I could breathe a little deeper now.

She had a great time in Arizona, and it seemed to reinvigorate her to both stay sober and move forward with her life. Having others her age who were also in recovery was something she deeply missed after moving back to Texas, and she loved the time she spent with them. It was also a nice break for me after everything that had happened since she'd moved home.

When she returned, we scheduled a "graduation" photo shoot to celebrate her earning her GED. Since there was no actual school involved, she chose a baby blue cap and gown from Amazon, and a few outfits to wear. We decided to add a recovery twist to her pictures, bringing along her AA chips and her monkey fist, symbols of sobriety. She bonded easily with the young woman photographer, who loved how photogenic she was. I think she took well over two hundred pictures! At the end of the session, she coaxed me into a few photos as well, which was fun, even though I was not at all expecting it. The experience was really nice, and we were absolutely thrilled with the resulting pictures.

Throughout the entire time since Regan first moved to Arizona, I had not been open with many people about our situation. Only those closest to me knew, including my family, and I was comfortable with it this way. I can't really explain what got into me as I typed a Facebook post to go along with thirty of our favorite photos:

> *Sometimes life doesn't go as planned. However, there can still be joy in the journey. This girl finished high school last month and we are celebrating her BIG!! She's coming up on sixteen months in recovery from substance abuse and she's so proud of herself, but I am amazed by her every day. I could have posted her pictures and left out the ones that incorporated her recovery and most people wouldn't have thought anything of it. She's gorgeous! But I couldn't do that in good faith. By the grace of God, she's alive and well and thriving and happy.*

This is what recovery can look like. We are incredibly grateful to be able to post these pictures and say to you that even though her journey was hard. Even though it wasn't what we wanted. Even though it seems ugly to the world. We are changed and we are blessed and we have found purpose on this road. As our photographer put it after taking these pictures, 'There's incredible power in owning your story.' Yes. Yes, there is. Here she is owning it and doing it beautifully Thank you Jesus for this girl and for our struggles. I will praise You all my days. Congratulations, Baby Girl!

It was July 12th. I hit the "post" button, immediately panicked, and shut my computer. Then, I closed up my office and headed home, all the while asking myself again, "*What have I done?*" The tears came as I drove the forty-five minutes home. Would people think badly of her? What if someone said something ugly and hurt her? Even though I'd gotten her permission to post the pictures, I regretted it. I would delete it as soon as I got home. I shouldn't have posted it and exposed her like that. Again, fear overtook me. Until I stopped to get gas about twenty minutes down the road, and saw that I had several notifications and messages. I read the first one parked at the gas pump. It was from her volleyball coach from junior high, and it was so beautiful and supportive, I cried more. More messages came and comments on my post from people whom we hadn't seen or talked to in years, and ALL were positive and supportive. I couldn't believe it. It was all out in the open now, and it was okay. Some shared that they, too, were going through a similar journey. For the first time, it occurred to me that sharing our experiences might be helpful to others who feel otherwise alone.

A few weeks later, I reached out to Josh, the owner of Pathway, to ask if he would let me start parent meetings in my area for other parents who needed support. He loved the idea and said he'd gladly let me do that, but also offered me another option to explore. There was a non-profit called PAL (Parents of Addicted Loved Ones) that he knew well, with a curriculum and free training for facilitators who wanted to offer support groups. I hadn't heard of them, but was excited to see what they were all about. After reading their website, I searched for meetings in/near Houston, TX.

There was not a single meeting within fifty miles of one of the largest cities in the country. I cried at this realization. Where do parents here go to get support and help with their addicted children? I wasted no time in reaching out to Josh's contact there, who replied to me within a couple of hours. I loved that their meetings were specifically designed for parents with addicted kids of any age, openly utilized the power of prayer, and offered educational topics in addition to sharing experiences. It took me about a week to complete the free online facilitator training, and I held the first PAL meeting in the Houston area on July 23rd. Now, in addition to attending the parent meetings at Pathway online each week for myself, I was giving others the gift of support with PAL. I started to sponsor other parents through my parent twelve-step meetings at Pathway simultaneously.

Over the next several months, growth seemed to progress slowly, although much was happening. Regan and I attended a process group at the recovery center she'd become a part of every Saturday morning together. These meetings were fun for me because I got the opportunity to be in a room with others who struggled with drug and alcohol addiction, and sometimes their significant others would also attend. Topics varied, and I got an inside look at my daughter's perspectives, which almost always impressed me.

Regan started a job as a caregiver for an older gentleman, with whom she quickly bonded. She loved making him laugh and listening to his stories about his life. She would stay with him from Friday afternoon through Monday morning most weekends. Later on, after the caregiving job ended due to the man's passing, she started working for her dad, doing some online tasks for a project he was involved with. Regan also researched and enrolled in cosmetology school that fall, graduating as an eyelash technician. Additionally, she completed the training to become a Certified Recovery Coach, hoping to work with others finding their way in recovery.

Since her relapse, Regan's relationship with Jacob had once again become mostly nonexistent. Whether he was angry at her for slipping up or simply caught up in his own life, she couldn't be sure. What she did know was that the brother who had once been her best friend now frequently ignored her calls and messages—sometimes responding days later, sometimes not at all. She tried to push through, giving him space while still hoping for some semblance of a connection, but the inconsistency became too painful to endure. For the sake of her mental health and sobriety, she made the difficult decision to step away. She wrote him an email, expressing what she needed from their relationship and how his absence was affecting her. He never responded. And just like that, their relationship was paused.

I knew how hard this was for her. She had always loved her brother deeply and wanted nothing more than to be close to him the way they had been as kids. But she also knew that the uncertainty of where she stood with him was becoming dangerous—one of the few things that could genuinely put her recovery at risk. As much as it hurt to watch, I was encouraged to see her prioritizing her own well-being and setting the boundaries she needed.

I understood the pain of that choice more than she probably realized. Two months earlier, my relationship with Jacob had once again been abruptly cut off—his decision, not mine. It was a silent loss I carried every day but one I rarely spoke about. Our experiences were different, but the heartbreak was the same. And through it all, our love for him never wavered.

Regan and I continued to grow close. I worked hard at relinquishing the "mom" role as she approached her nineteenth birthday, focusing on treating her as a capable adult. We had a lot of opportunities to talk, and we grew closer and closer over time. In late July, we had the opportunity to do an interview with Melissa Radke for her *Ordinary People, Ordinary Things* podcast. The episode dropped in November and was titled "All in the Family." That fall, we did a few other podcast interviews as well, telling our story together, hoping to offer hope to other families with similar struggles. We also spoke at a community meeting held at the recovery center, where we'd been attending meetings on Saturday mornings. There, I met the man who would become my employer and change my professional path completely.

I was trained as a certified IASIS MicroCurrent Neurofeedback provider in August and began working for a non-profit that helped people with substance use disorder in recovery. The microcurrent neurofeedback system I used facilitates brain rebalancing and improves performance, effectively helping with many mental, emotional, and physical conditions, including addiction. While it doesn't help someone decide to be sober, it does help many of the underlying causal factors that lead addicts to use drugs and alcohol as a way to cope, such as depression, anxiety, insomnia, PTSD, and chronic pain. As a new provider, I needed people to practice on, so I was allowed to treat Regan for free. This turned out to be an incredible gift, as it helped alleviate all of her issues with headaches, neck pain, sleep, anxiety, and feeling "flat" (a common condition in early sobriety as the dopamine threshold moves back down to normal). After her first session, she sent me a message on her drive home telling me she hadn't felt this happy in a very long time. She came for weekly sessions for about four months, helping me practice and reaping the amazing benefits of healing.

As many opportunities and gifts as we were given from God during this first year of recovery, things weren't perfect. I struggled with trusting Regan, especially when she would be out late with friends. I would panic and call and text her to find out where she was and what she was doing, none of which was ever my business. There was nothing she would decide to do or not do that was in my control. Still, I struggled with worrying about her, and each time I called her to find out if she was okay, I knew I shouldn't be.

This was another pivotal moment—not just for Regan, but for me. Eventually, she confronted me about my behavior. While I knew she had to be annoyed by my constant check-ins, she never lashed out or acted exasperated. Instead, she showed me grace, always making sure to let me know she was okay, where she was, who she was with, and when she'd be home. But she had reached her limit.

"Mom, I know you worry, but I need you to trust me," she said one evening, her voice calm but firm.

Her words stung—not because they were harsh, but because they were true. I was suffocating her with my anxiety, unable to fully release the grip I had on my fear. She wasn't doing anything wrong. She wasn't disappearing without a word. Yet, my panic-stricken calls and texts sent the message that I still didn't fully trust her. The realization was humbling.

I apologized, promising I would do better. She, in turn, offered to be more proactive about updating me if she was going to be out later than planned. It was a small compromise, but one that made a difference.

It's not easy to be called out by your own child, but she was right—I needed to stop living in fear. I wrote a reminder on my bathroom mirror that I found online. The author is unknown, but the words were meaningful to me: "There is not enough room in your mind for both worry and faith. You must decide which one gets to live there." I chose faith. I chose to trust my daughter. But the truth was, this wasn't a one-time decision. It was a choice I would have to make over and over again before I was truly able to let go.

Six months after her nineteenth birthday, we celebrated Regan's one year of sobriety. This milestone was huge, and we marked the occasion by getting matching tattoos. She'd taken up painting while at Pathway and was pretty good at it. After her relapse, she painted a beautiful butterfly with blue and violet watercolor wings opposite one another, while the complementary wings were left blank. The meaning behind the painting depicts the color returning to her wings through her recovery, and the absence of color represents how empty she felt when she was using. The butterfly itself is a symbol of growth and transformation. We both felt it was the perfect tattoo to symbolize all that we'd been through.

It took four hours for each tattoo to be recreated on our right forearms, making us almost late to her celebration dinner at The Cheesecake Factory. More than twenty friends joined us in celebrating her accomplishment, complete with gifts and custom-made cookies marking the occasion. I had contacted family members, friends, and counselors at Pathway, asking each one to send me a video of themselves to share with her on her big day. They came through, and I put together all the sentiments into one video, gifting it to her at dinner. She loved it so much, crying through all fifteen minutes of it, especially when her beloved counselor, Merrillee, began talking. Regan's comment to me after listening to Merrillee's words was, "I wouldn't be here if it wasn't for her."

I knew this was true. Regan was voted least likely to remain sober during her time at Pathway. She was a tough case, tougher than I'd ever known. It took two years to reach one year of continuous sobriety, and we relished in the accomplishment, but mostly, we celebrated her life—the life she had planned to extinguish by the time she turned eighteen. There was much to be thankful for, but there was still work to be done.

REGAN

My faith journey took a lot of twists and turns while I was at Pathway and even after that. Growing up, I believed in God, went to church every Sunday with my mom and brother, and later with Tim when he became part of our family. I prayed every night, especially during junior high and the beginning of high school, always asking God to fix things in my family. But instead of getting better, everything kept getting worse. Over time, I started to resent Him. By the time I started using drugs, I wasn't just frustrated—I was angry. I didn't believe in Him anymore. If He was real, where had He been? He clearly wasn't there for me.

At Pathway, the Twelve Step program made a big deal about having a "Higher Power," and my counselors kept pushing me to find one. They wanted me to believe in God—or at least something greater than myself. I wasn't interested. I told them straight up that I didn't believe in God, that He wasn't real, and sometimes, I'd even say I hated Him. Merrillee caught on to that last part and hit me with something I wasn't expecting: "You can't hate something that isn't real." As much as I didn't want to admit it, she was right—again. That messed with me a little. I stopped saying God wasn't real, but still felt abandoned by Him. If He was really there, then why had He never had my back?

Even though I was skeptical, my counselors kept pushing me to try praying. At first, I wanted nothing to do with it, but eventually, I gave in. And over time, I noticed that praying actually made me feel a little more at peace, even a little happier. But I didn't start off praying to God. Instead, I talked to Bre. She was my old neighbor and childhood friend who had died when I was a freshman. She had always felt like an older sister to me, and I saw her as an angel. So, I started having little conversations with her, and that's how I eased into praying. Eventually, I started including God—the father of Jesus—in my prayers, but I still wasn't about to let anyone tie me to a religion.

I don't like being called a Christian, even though I do believe in Christ. The way I see it, Christianity—at least the way I've experienced it—is all about going to church and listening to preachers tell you their version of what the Bible means. A lot of those interpretations don't sit right with me. Some churches act like certain things automatically send you to hell—like being gay, dancing, or even cutting your hair. That never made sense to me. If I'm going to follow God, I want to understand His Word for myself. That's why I read the Bible on my own and trust what He tells me instead of just going along with what people say I'm supposed to believe.

I see God as loving and forgiving, and I believe that the only sin that truly condemns someone is blasphemy. What's always been hard for me, though, is seeing people who call themselves Christians act in ways that are hurtful or hypocritical. That's made me really hesitant to associate myself with a religion that sometimes feels more focused on judgment than on actual faith.

Once I let go of all the anger I had toward God, I started focusing on having a real, personal relationship with Him—one that actually felt meaningful to me. I don't think I need to go to church to make that happen. I'd rather connect with Him on my own, in the comfort of my own home, without all the expectations or rules that people try to attach to religion. For me, faith is personal. It's between me and Him, and that's all that matters.

After my relapse, my faith became a much bigger part of my recovery. I also reconnected with my Pathway friends and started going to a local women's AA group. The women there were nice and welcoming, but they were older, and at eighteen, I had a hard time relating to them the way I could with my friends from Pathway. Still, I kept going as often as I could, partly because I wanted to stay on track but also because I didn't want to lose the connections I had worked so hard to rebuild. FaceTiming with my Pathway friends every day helped a lot. They were the ones who really understood me, and soon enough, I was itching to go back to Arizona and see them again.

Earning my GED gave me a huge confidence boost. I didn't think it would mean that much to me, but accomplishing that—then getting to celebrate it with my Arizona friends when I visited—made me feel like I was actually moving forward in my life. It made me want to keep finding things that gave me joy and purpose. Through all of it, Sofi was always there. I felt a huge responsibility to make up for everything she had been through because of me. She was my constant, and I wanted to create a better future for both of us.

When I decided to go public with my story, I did it because I wanted to help other people. But I'd be lying if I said I wasn't scared. I worried that people from my past would come out of nowhere and have something negative to say, just like they had before. But I also knew that I couldn't control what people thought of me. What mattered was that I was proud of how far I'd come. Sharing my story became part of my healing, and I chose to focus on the good it could do instead of the fear of being judged.

I loved my job taking care of Ken. It didn't even feel like work—he was like an old friend with the best stories. Every time I was with him, I felt like I was learning something. When I told him about my addiction and my recovery, he didn't judge me at all. Instead, he encouraged me and told me how proud he was. That meant a lot to me. He really supported me in a way that felt genuine, and I think that's when I realized how much I enjoyed working with the elderly. When he passed away, it was really hard. I missed him a lot, but I also felt so grateful for the time I had with him. I knew he had lived a long, full life, and I was lucky to have been a small part of it.

That summer, I was sitting outside by the pool when my mom showed me a text conversation she had with Jacob. She had sent him an update about me—how I had graduated, my plans to go to cosmetology school, her new job, and even the interview we did with Melissa Radke. His response? "If I really cared, I'd ask."

I lost it. I was instantly pissed off. It wasn't even directed at me, but it might as well have been. It was just another reminder of how much he didn't care. I sat down and typed out a long email to him. I didn't hold back. I called him out for acting like he was better than everyone else, like he was somehow above our family, when, in reality, none of us were perfect. I reminded him how much I had put up with from him—how I had loved him through everything, kept his secrets, and worked so hard to maintain our relationship, and for what?

I listed all the ways he had hurt me and everything I had gone through while he just ignored me. Then I asked him straight-up: Did he even care? Did he ever notice? At the end of it, I told him that until he actually took the time to heal or do some real soul-searching, I didn't want anything to do with him unless it could be a healthy relationship. He never responded. I didn't feel bad about sending it, though. I meant every word.

At the same time, I started spending more time at the local recovery center. It reminded me of "the shop" at Pathway—a place where I could just be. There wasn't anyone my age, but I didn't really care. The meetings there were way better than the AA meetings I'd been going to, and over time, I started making friends. It became my safe place, somewhere I could go when I needed to get out of the house and just be around people who understood.

At first, I was pretty skeptical about the new treatment my mom had started offering—MicroCurrent Neurofeedback. It honestly sounded weird, and I wasn't convinced it would do anything. But I figured it couldn't hurt, so I made the drive to Houston for my first session. To my surprise, I felt different almost immediately. I left feeling lighter and happier, and, for the first time in a long time, I didn't have that nagging craving to get high.

As I kept going to sessions, the changes became even more noticeable. My anxiety and depression, which had been a constant part of my life, started to ease—and then, they were just gone. I was sleeping better, I wasn't overthinking everything, and I didn't have to force myself to be happy anymore. I actually felt happy. It was real. I felt like *me* again.

Later that fall, I reached out to Olivia. I had thought about it for a while, but kept hesitating. She had still been close with the high school friend group that treated me like s***, and I wasn't sure if I wanted to open that door. But over time, I saw her start to drift away from them, and eventually, she left them behind completely. When we reconnected, I told her everything—about my drug use, about my family, about all the things I had been through. And she was just… Olivia. No judgment. No hesitation. Just love and support, like she'd always been.

We started hanging out again, and by the time February rolled around, I was staying with her for a week while taking my Recovery Coaching Certification course. Her boyfriend was out of town, and I remember getting to her place that first night and finding her *sobbing*. She had just found out he cheated on her—with one of the girls from our old high school friend group.

I didn't even think—I grabbed a trash bag and marched to her closet. "You're done with him," I told her, and we started packing up all his crap. That night, we drove all the way to Magnolia, where he was staying, and dumped his stuff right in the middle of the road. I remember thinking, *this is personal*. I knew exactly what it felt like to be betrayed, and I *wasn't* going to let him make her feel like she was nothing. That night changed everything. She was already my best friend, but from that moment on, we were inseparable.

Just a couple of weeks later, I celebrated my one-year sober anniversary. I had been waiting for this moment and *needed* a tattoo to mark it. Mom got one, too. I thought I had plenty of time before my dinner, but of course, it took longer than expected. By the time I got to The Cheesecake Factory—my absolute favorite restaurant—everyone was already there, waiting for me.

The best part of the night was the video. I sat there watching messages from all of my favorite people, and it made me emotional in a way I wasn't expecting. Mama Maureen's message was beautiful, but then I saw *Merrillee*, and that one hit me the hardest. Seeing her face, hearing her words—it meant *everything*. I felt so incredibly loved.

Painting had been my outlet for a long time—first in high school, then at Pathway, and even after I moved home. Most recently, I had been painting butterflies. It just felt right. One painting became the tattoo that Mom and I got on our forearms to commemorate my sober anniversary. I didn't plan the design when I painted it, but it ended up being a butterfly with both empty and colored wings opposite each other. The empty wings represented my past—my addiction and all the painful stuff I had been through. The two colorful wings represented the beauty, happiness, and hope I had now that I was sober. My butterfly painting was more than just art; it was a reflection of my life story—the pain, the growth, and the transformation.

Chapter 11
Success

After celebrating Regan's one year of sobriety, the world shut down due to the COVID-19 pandemic. We often talked about how grateful we were to have been able to host her party before the lockdown kept us all confined to our homes the following day. During those months, I interviewed Regan on our back porch about her experiences in treatment. We called the series "Regan Talks Rehab" and posted it on a website called *Our Beautiful Recovery*. We also hosted Facebook Live Q&A sessions, even featuring Josh Azevedo from Pathway as a guest. Our hope was to reach other families in similar situations, offering them hope and resources.

During this time, Regan spent months painting a mural at the recovery center, where we attended meetings. She stenciled the Twelve Steps and Twelve Traditions on one of its large walls, surrounded by giant butterflies, planets, recovery symbols, bluebonnets, and the iconic Houston "Be Someone" overpass. The mural was stunning and showcased her artistic talent. I would join her in the evenings, working on the stenciling while she handled the detailed artwork. Painting together became a comforting ritual, filled with laughter, singing along to oldies music, and chatting until we cleaned our brushes and headed home.

I continued to host Parents of Addicted Loved Ones meetings and attend virtually the Pathway parent meetings each week. While Regan was growing and thriving, I was also finding my own footing in this new chapter of life. After eight months of working as an IASIS MicroCurrent Neurofeedback provider, I decided to pursue my chemical dependency counseling license. Seeing clients had opened my eyes to the emotional weight many carried—grown men and women often cried in my office, sharing deeply personal stories they had never told anyone before. I found purpose in being a trusted confidante, and when my license finally arrived just before Christmas, it felt like an early gift. I also launched my own private practice, offering addiction counseling and IASIS Micro-Current Neurofeedback, which I named The Mind Connection.

At around twenty months of sobriety, Regan was invited to share her story on the *Let's Talk Recovery* podcast. Preparing for the interview brought up mixed emotions for her as she wrestled with how much to disclose about the abuse she had endured from her dad and brother. She feared their reactions but also felt a responsibility to be truthful about her experiences. In the end, she navigated the interview with grace, balancing honesty with diplomacy. While I'm not sure her dad ever listened to it, she did an incredible job, and I couldn't have been prouder of her.

That fall, Regan took a bold step by enrolling in classes at the local community college to pursue a career as a chemical dependency counselor. This was a significant milestone—she had never believed she was smart enough for college, and her decision to pursue this path made me immensely proud. Her own life experiences and young age gave her a unique ability to connect with teens and young adults, and I knew she would make an incredible counselor.

Regan continued working online for her dad part-time while attending college. One of her visits to Arizona was before Christmas that year, and she planned to spend about a week with her friends in Phoenix and a week with her dad in Cottonwood. Kyle (Boomer) at Pathway had asked her to speak at a parent meeting during her trip as well. She found out when she arrived that the meeting she would be speaking at was during the time she'd planned to be at her dad's. Knowing it would be inconvenient, she let him know her plans. He told her he would be able to get her to Pathway for the meeting, and she started planning what she would say to the parents who had once been so kind and supportive of her.

When she went to stay with her dad, she felt not good enough for him from the moment she arrived. He planned for her to accompany him to church, but complained about what she'd brought to wear. He also didn't like her hair and wondered why she was so skinny. Nothing she did was right, but he refused to go to church without her. She was hurt and angry by his comments, but she was stuck there until at least Thursday, so she did her best to just make it through. Her dad drove her halfway to Phoenix on Thursday afternoon, where they met a friend of hers who drove her the rest of the way to Pathway in time for the meeting.

This arrangement at the last minute effectively opted him out of watching her speak. She called to tell me she'd gotten there and that her dad hadn't come with her. Even after everything, I couldn't believe he wasn't jumping at the chance to support her. I couldn't hide my disappointment for her, but I encouraged her as best as I could: "You're going to be amazing." I think she appreciated the reassurance, even if it couldn't make up for his absence.

I attended the meeting virtually and was blown away by how

confidently she addressed the parents, sharing her recovery journey. They asked thoughtful questions, particularly about how she managed her sobriety with her family living so far away. She seemed at ease in front of the group, and they were captivated by her story. Afterward, she lingered at Pathway, catching up with friends and parents who had always supported her. She called me, conflicted about returning to her dad's house. She didn't want to go. Ultimately, a friend drove her back later that night.

Regan stayed at her dad's for just another day before telling him she had plans with friends who were coming to pick her up. Though he seemed disappointed, she left anyway, relieved to be back in Phoenix with people who made her feel accepted. That trip would be the last time she saw her dad for five years, though she continued working for him after returning home.

After the holidays, while Regan was spending time with Olivia, someone cut off and stole the catalytic converter from her car. The beloved "toaster" now roared like a chainsaw, and though we couldn't help but laugh at her embarrassment driving it around, it was a frustrating situation. When her insurance company deemed the car a total loss, they gave her a payout to put toward a replacement. She was heartbroken to part with the toaster, which held so many memories from her time at Pathway. Still, she approached the process of buying a new car with determination.

She consulted her dad, who was knowledgeable about the car industry, and also came to Tim and me for advice on choosing the right car and negotiating with salespeople. After test-driving a few cars on her own, she quickly found the perfect fit: a white 2017 Honda Accord with low miles. It was within the budget her dad had recommended, and it had everything she wanted. Tim and I accompanied her to the dealership to help with the financing and paperwork. Thanks to the payout from her insurance, she was able to put down a large amount, securing an affordable payment. Her dad had also promised her at least twenty hours of work per week, which gave her the confidence to commit to the purchase. We took photos of her proudly standing beside her new car before she drove it off the lot that night, excited for this next chapter of independence.

But within weeks, Regan realized she was barely getting any hours from her dad. Worried she wouldn't have enough money to make her first car payment, she came to me for advice. Surprised, I encouraged her to reach out to him, reminding her that he had made a clear promise to provide consistent work. I'd even over-heard him say it, so I felt confident they could resolve the issue. Despite her nerves, she brought it up with him, only to learn the shocking truth: he had hired someone else to do her job for less money! Whether he believed she had quit or had outright decided to fire her was unclear, but the effect was the same.

This was a defining moment for Regan. When she confronted him, he dismissed her concerns, questioning why she had chosen such a nice car in the first place. His words stung, a casual disre-gard for the commitment he had made to her. But Regan didn't waste time dwelling on the hurt. Instead, she channeled her ener-gy into finding a new job, determined to stand on her own. Still, something had shifted. This wasn't just about a broken promise—it was about a pattern she could no longer ignore. At that moment, a quiet resolve settled in. She would never count on her dad for anything again.

YEAR 3 AND BEYOND

Not long after her second sober anniversary, Regan asked me if I knew any counselors she could talk to. I was only mildly sur-prised and asked her what kind of therapy she was looking for.

She explained she was ready to work through the trauma she had endured with her dad growing up. The pain still weighed on her, and she feared it might cause her to relapse one day. I thought of a counselor I'd recently met who practiced brainspotting, a therapeutic technique designed to help clients process trauma.

I passed along her contact information to Regan. They connected at least three times, and the experience seemed to have a profound effect. I remember Regan telling me that in the first session, although there had been no talking, she'd cried the entire ninety minutes and felt drained of energy for the rest of the afternoon and evening. Yet, she described a weight being lifted, and the memories that had haunted her no longer carried the same emotional charge. Watching her take this brave step toward healing made me so proud. I had always wished I could take her pain away, but I knew this was something she had to face on her own.

Regan quickly got a job working for James Avery, a popular jewelry company. Around the same time, I had gone to a networking meeting nearby to promote my new business. I met a woman who ran an adolescent recovery group that had some similarities to Pathway. I mentioned that my daughter had attended a program in Arizona and was currently two years sober and working on becoming a chemical dependency counselor. She immediately gave me her card, telling me to have her contact her if she wanted a job. "Wow," I thought, "What a perfect opportunity for her!"

When I told her about the opportunity, she wasn't as excited as I'd hoped. She felt unsure, and besides, she already had a job. I gave her the card and the information and encouraged her to think about it. Within a short time, I believe God stepped in. She wasn't getting enough hours at James Avery to pay her car payment and insurance, so she needed more income. I reminded her of the recovery group, and she finally gave the woman a call. After a couple of interviews, she was offered a job as an assistant with the group on the north side of Houston. She ran meetings, drove kids around, planned fun events, and coordinated everything for them. Soon, she was promoted to handle a much larger group in Houston. She put in long hours, well into the evenings, five days each week. The kids loved her, and the parents appreciated her even more. She was in her element with those kids, acting as a friend, mentor, recovery coach, and challenging them hard when they'd get out of line. The amount of personal growth I got to witness during the eighteen months she worked there was nothing short of inspiring.

About six months after starting this job, Regan decided that she was tired of having a disingenuous relationship with her dad. I don't know if he did or said something that triggered this or if she'd been pondering the situation for a while. After the situation with the car, their communication had dwindled, and she seemed to view him in a new light. She decided to write him an email, much like the one she had sent her brother the year before. In the email, she expressed a desire for a deeper, more genuine relationship with him but made it clear that this would require accountability on his part. She listed specific ways his actions had hurt her and asked him to acknowledge the pain he had caused.

His response sidestepped responsibility and instead subtly placed blame on her for their difficult relationship. Regan, now armed with confidence and self-respect, responded with an email that pulled no punches. She detailed his behavior, his character, and the damage caused by his attempts to destroy her mother (me). She poured out everything she had held in for years, believing that if he were ever to have a place in her life, the truth needed to be addressed. He never replied to that email, and their relationship remained on pause for the next few years.

There are moments in life when addressing unhealthy relationships—especially with family—becomes necessary. It takes immense courage and strength to confront these dynamics and set boundaries, and Regan was proving she had both. By demanding better for herself, she demonstrated incredible personal growth. Watching her take back her power left me in awe. Though she grieved the loss of those relationships, she resolved to put herself first. At just twenty-one years old, she displayed wisdom and boldness far beyond her years.

At the same time, my business was rapidly growing. After speaking with a few trusted counselors, I decided to pursue my master's degree and become a licensed professional counselor. I felt a deep calling to work with clients, especially those impacted by addiction. Everything I had learned and experienced on this journey made me realize that if I could share something that might help even one person, it would be worth it.

Around the time of her three-year sober anniversary, Regan decided it was time to move out of our home. While I wasn't thrilled to see her go, I respected that she was in charge of her own life. We searched for apartments together, and she chose a charming one-bedroom in a safe complex located roughly halfway between her job in Houston and our house. She was efficient—signing the lease within a few days. Tim helped her move into her third-floor apartment while I was at work, and the next day, I joined her to finish unpacking and add a few decorative touches. The space turned out beautifully, and she was thrilled to live independently with Sofi. Our house felt strangely quiet again, but this time, for all the right reasons.

During this season of transition, Regan also decided it was finally time to complete her Twelve Step work. Despite being in recovery for several years, she had never finished all the steps with a sponsor. There were a variety of reasons for this—sometimes her lack of motivation, and other times, a sponsor who didn't stick around long enough. Determined to see it through, she chose Rachel, a woman twenty years older whom she'd connected with in the recovery community. Rachel was eager to help her succeed, but also committed to holding her accountable. By the summer, they had worked through most of the steps, reaching Step Nine: "Make direct amends to such people wherever possible, except when to do so would injure them or others."

I don't know much about Regan's amends list, but her brother, Jacob, was on it. When Rachel insisted that she reach out to him, Regan was hesitant. "I can't," she said, explaining that Jacob had blocked her on every platform. Rachel, however, wouldn't let her off the hook. "Where there's a will, there's a way," she said, challenging Regan to figure it out.

Through a mutual friend, who graciously acted as an intermediary, Regan was able to get her number unblocked. She then scheduled a day and time to call him. When he answered, she asked him to simply listen as she read her amends letter. I knew how nervous she was—rightly so—but she summoned her courage and spoke her heart. That phone call lasted nearly three hours and seemed to mark the beginning (once again) of their relationship. Regan felt cautiously hopeful after the conversation, encouraged by how well it had gone. However, the progress was short-lived. Before long, their communication dwindled once more, fading into infrequent contact.

The following summer, a bit out of nowhere, Regan came to me with unexpected news: she wanted to work alongside me as an IASIS MicroCurrent Neurofeedback provider. Having experienced its profound impact on her own healing, she wanted to offer that same help to others. Her request caught me off guard.

"You want to work with me?" I asked, unsure if I'd heard her correctly.

"Yes! I mean… if you'd be okay with it," she replied, her voice a mix of eagerness and nerves.

At the time, she was nearing the end of her position with the adolescent recovery group, preparing to apply for her counseling license and ready for the next chapter in her journey. I hadn't envisioned adding someone to my practice—let alone my daughter—but my initial surprise gave way to gratitude as I thought about her offer. The chance to work alongside Regan felt nothing short of miraculous. I couldn't have imagined this moment just a few years ago, but here we were. *This is You, God. Thank you.*

I sent her to training, and she shadowed me in sessions for an entire month. I poured into her everything I had learned from three years of working with clients, but she quickly demonstrated her own natural abilities—an intuitive understanding of people and an innate sense of how to help them heal. Within six months, The Mind Connection had outgrown its previous space, and we moved into a new building with our name on the marquee. Together, we expanded our services and welcomed more clients than ever before. Her fresh perspective and creative ideas have helped us grow, and I truly couldn't ask for a better partner. She is also my closest friend.

Shortly after the move, Regan relocated to a new, larger apartment closer to the office. Her confidence continued to grow, and within a year, she enrolled at a university to pursue her dream of earning a doctorate in psychology. Today, she balances her work with classes and celebrates over six years of sobriety—a milestone that reminds me daily of the extraordinary journey we've traveled together.

I continue to facilitate weekly PAL (Parents of Addicted Loved Ones) meetings in my office waiting room—offering parents like me a refuge of hope. In May 2024, I achieved a milestone I once could only dream of: graduating with my Master of Education in Clinical Mental Health Counseling and obtaining my professional counseling license shortly after.

On January 11, 2020, I made a life-altering decision to give up alcohol, no longer willing to partake in something that could have, and maybe should have, taken my daughter from this world. Today, I live and work with integrity, embracing sobriety as a reflection of the very principles I share with others in the addiction and recovery field.

This journey—walking through the fire of addiction and emerging into the light of recovery alongside my daughter—has transformed me in ways I never imagined. And despite the pain and heartache, I wouldn't trade it for anything.

"I have told you these things, so that in me you may have peace. In this world you will have trouble. But take heart! I have overcome the world" (John 16:33).

REGAN

After I hit my one-year sobriety milestone, my confidence started growing with every new accomplishment—big or small. Starting college and doing brainspotting therapy felt like my first real effort to focus on my own healing. For the first time, I actually wanted to let go of the weight of my past trauma instead of just pushing it aside. I also started putting more thought into what I wanted to do with my life, and no matter what direction I considered, helping others was always at the forefront.

In one of my counseling classes, I wrote a paper that was really personal and vulnerable. When I got it back, my professor had given me an A, but she also attached a note saying how much my paper had impacted her. She told me she really admired my strength and suggested that I look into brainspotting therapy to work through some of the trauma I'd written about. I let her know that I had already done brainspotting and that it had helped me more than I could explain. That conversation really stuck with me, and about a year later, my mom and I took the training to offer brainspotting to our clients at The Mind Connection.

Around that same time, I had a phone call with my dad that completely caught me off guard. My work hours had been really slow, and my car payment was coming up, so I casually mentioned that I had gotten a business card from a woman who ran an adolescent recovery group and that they were looking to hire someone. Before I even finished my sentence, he got super excited. "That's wonderful! That sounds like a great opportunity for you!" But then, in almost the same breath, he added, "It's great timing, too, because I actually hired someone else to do your job since it was cheaper."

I felt like I'd been stabbed in the back. I don't even remember what I said after that—I just ended the call as fast as I could so I could process what had just happened.

I ended up working at James Avery for a few months, but they cut everyone's hours because they had overhired. So, I finally reached out to the woman at Cornerstone, the adolescent recovery group, and immediately set up an interview. I got the job on the spot. At first, I tried to juggle both jobs, but when James Avery refused to work around my schedule at Cornerstone, I quit.

Working at Cornerstone was exactly the kind of experience I wanted. It was in line with my career goals, and I loved the kids in the program—even though they drove me absolutely crazy. I understood them, and that's what made me so good at my job.

The long hours made it tough to balance work and school, but I wouldn't trade that experience for anything.

When I joined my mom at The Mind Connection, I kept pushing myself forward. I had to figure out how to grow my own business and navigate a career path on my own. I don't work under my mom—I'm an independent practitioner—which means I have to make sure I stay educated and up-to-date on the latest trends and research in my field. It's a lot of responsibility, but I love the freedom of working for myself.

Going back to school and working toward my doctorate feels like a huge accomplishment. One of the best parts about running my own business is the flexibility—I can give my energy to both my clients and my studies without feeling stretched too thin. Plus, I get to bring my dog to work with me every day, which honestly makes everything better.

More than anything, I'm proud of my perseverance—just continuing to do the next right thing, putting one foot in front of the other, and always moving forward. I'm still learning new things about myself, about life, and about the world I want to create for myself and others. I stay open to opportunities that align with my values and follow where they lead me. There's no finish line, no point where I'll ever feel like I'm done, and there's nothing left to accomplish.

At the end of the day, besides helping people, all I really want is to be happy and have a peaceful life. I don't have the tolerance for negativity or drama—I had enough of that when I was younger. I guess you could say I have a low pain tolerance, but really, I just have a low threshold for anything that doesn't serve me. Every accomplishment, every step forward, is shaping the life I want for myself. And that's what matters.

Epilogue

It was my sincere hope that once this book was written and published, I could say that our family had also received a miracle—the miracle of restoration. While that has not happened, there are some glimmers of hope, and I remain steadfast that God continues to work on our behalf.

My relationship with Regan is as solid as it has ever been. We have shared so much and worked so hard to repair our relationship, even the parts that I hadn't known were broken. I've worked hard at treating her like the capable adult young woman that she is, and we've formed a healthy and close friendship as two adults over the last several years. She is a light in not only my world but also to all who know her. I will always be her biggest cheerleader and encourager, and I am grateful for all that she has taught me.

Jacob has remained estranged from me since that summer in 2019, after that text message I showed Regan by the pool. We have only shared a few emails since that time, and they were not conducive to reconciliation on his end. Recently, after five years of silence, I received an email from him completely out of the blue. It simply said he loves me and wanted me to know that. I wrote him back the same. Maybe the door is cracked open. I don't know for sure. I miss him beyond words and pray endlessly that he will change his mind and want to include me in his life. But for now, I cling to the hope of Jesus and the promise that all things are possible through Christ, who strengthens me (Philippians 4:13). And I wait.

My relationship with my ex-husband has been non-existent since mid-2021. We have had no contact with one another and really no reason to. Our children are adults, and our relationships are our own to navigate. I have no ill will toward him and have forgiven him for the things he did and said to our children a long time ago. Vengeance is not mine, and I have no use for it. I hope he can live peacefully with his choices, and if he can't, that he will make restitution to our children or others who were also harmed. They deserve it.

I leave you with this excerpt from Beth Moore's *Entrusted* Bible Study:

> When we run into great difficulty or pain in the journey of our calling, we're prone to either cast blame or jump to the conclusion that we must have done something wrong or landed somewhere wrong in our attempt to discern God's will. **But sometimes hardship will come because you got it right.** As hard as this is to grasp, sometimes suffering bubbles up from the well of God's immeasurable affection and devotion to us. He is not unfeeling. He is all-knowing. Something down the road depends on our present stretch of pave-

```
ment. This He promises us: the
suffering will be brief, and the
fruit of it as long as eternity
(2 Corinthians 4:17).²
```

REGAN

My relationship with Tim has only grown closer over the years, and honestly, I wish I could spend even more time with him. He is one of the most special people in my life—he's always been there when I needed him most. His unwavering support and protection have shown me, time and time again, that he has my back no matter what. I still feel guilty sometimes, knowing that out of everyone, he deserved all of the chaos the least. But despite everything, he stayed. And the fact that he chose to stay and love me, even when things were really hard, has proven to me that I am worth more than I ever believed. He is one of the biggest reasons I know my value, and I thank God all the time for blessing me with him.

A little over a year ago, I reconnected with my dad. For the first time, we've been able to have deeper, more meaningful conversations—something that never really happened before. So far, our relationship is going well, and I feel grateful to have him in my life. At the same time, I'm cautious. I'm taking things at my own pace, moving in a way that feels safe and comfortable for me. More than anything, I'm determined to keep our relationship on terms that contribute to my peace and happiness. I'll never compromise myself again just to make it work.

It's been a similar situation with Jacob. We don't talk as consistently as I do with my dad, but I'm happy that he's back in my life. Seeing him in person recently, alongside my dad, gave me a mo-

---

² Moore, Beth. *Entrusted: A Study of 2 Timothy*. LifeWay Press, 2016.

ment of clarity. I realized just how much my relationship with Jacob has always held power over me—how much I've let him define my sense of well-being. It would be easy for me to fall back into old patterns, making him the center of my world again. But now, I see how important it is to let go of that dynamic. It's not about cutting him out of my life but about protecting my own well-being and learning to detach in a healthy way. I'm still figuring out how to navigate our relationship, and I truly hope for the best. But no matter what happens, I know I'll be okay.

Through everything, I am beyond grateful for the relationship I have with my mom. Despite any ups and downs, our bond is something I'll always cherish—whether we're spending time together, talking, or even working side by side as business partners. But more than anything, the one thing that means the most to me is knowing, without a doubt, that I always have her unwavering support. That kind of assurance is more meaningful than anything else. She has been the most and, at times, the only consistent source of love and encouragement in my life. And for that, I am forever grateful.

Sofi is still the center of my world, but now she has a new little sister—Sybil. I think about how different my healing journey would have been if I hadn't gotten Sofi when I did. The love of a dog is truly unmatched, and I know that both Sofi and Sybil have played a huge role in helping me find joy and purpose as I continue moving forward in my recovery.

Resources By Chapter

Chapter 6—
The Pathway Program
https://thepathwayprogram.com/

Chapter 7—
Beyond the Yellow Brick Road
By Bob Meehan and Tim Conway (2000) – Available on Amazon

Parent to Parent
By Susan Furtney (2012) – Available on Amazon

Al Anon
https://al-anon.org/

Chapter 10—
Alcoholics Anonymous
https://www.aa.org/the-big-book

Find an AA Meeting
https://www.aa.org/find-aa

Parents of Addicted Loved Ones
https://palgroup.org/

Chapter 11—
IASIS MicroCurrent Neurofeedback
https://microcurrentneurofeedback.com/

The Mind Connection
https://www.tmcbrainhealthcenter.com/

Brainspotting
https://brainspotting.com/

Epilogue—
Entrusted: A Study of 2 Timothy
By Beth Moore (2016) – Available on Amazon

Additional Helpful Resources I Recommend—

High Achiever
By Tiffany Jenkins (2019) – Available on Amazon

The Language of Letting Go: Daily Meditations on Codependency
By Melody Beattie (2009) – Available on Amazon

The Neurobiology of Addiction: Addiction 101 in Olson
YouTube, uploaded Sept. 19, 2017
https://youtu.be/ras8yOq30WY?si=5FElZJrJP1WNd-pd

The Greatest Miracle in the World
By Og Mandino (1975) – Available on Amazon

The Mastery of Love: A Practical Guide to the Art of Relationship
By Don Miguel Ruiz with Janet Mills (2010) – Available on Amazon